Nonprofit NONSENSE

How to Survive and Thrive in the Crazy World of Nonprofit Business

JENNIFER L. MAHER

ILLUSTRATIONS BY Rob Husberg

Published by

THE CAUSE ACADEMY®

ISBN: 978-0-9895357-0-0
Printed in the United States of America.

Published by
The Cause Academy, LLC
www.thecauseacademy.com

Book Cover Design by Steven Plummer
Book Formatting & Design by Andrea Leljak
Editing by Jeanine L'Ecuyer Communications and Scott Seckel

Love to my family who supported my wild writing frenzy, and to all the mentors in my life who encouraged me to set goals, raise my arms to the heavens, and achieve.
Thank you.

Jennifer Maher

For Mom, thank you for everything.

Rob Husberg

CONTENTS

ILLUSTRATIONS

ACKNOWLEDGEMENTS

"We become smarter through the wisdom of many."
Jennifer Maher

Special thanks to Nicole Buratovich, Jeanine L'Ecuyer, Scott Seckel and Andrea Leljak for the endless reads, and to the talented Rob Husberg for turning my amateur stick drawings and punch lines into the brilliant illustrations herein.

Thank you to my friends who shared with me their war stories, lessons learned, and sense of humor that made this book possible. I enjoyed combining your experiences with mine, imagining characters, and, at times, combining unrelated or fictitious happenings to make the lessons poignant and helpful.

Finally, to my nonprofit colleagues, my deep respect and gratitude for your daily work and dedication to making the world a better place. You are angels on earth, and I am honored to work among you.

MANAGING THE CRAZY

"Life can only be understood backwards;
but it must be lived forwards."

Søren Kierkegaard

For years, friends encouraged me to write a book about the nonprofit industry and my personal experiences. I just couldn't see it. The thought of supplying the world with yet another textbook on nonprofit management… Yuck. I fell asleep just thinking about it.

Then, a colleague and I were reminiscing about the hilarious situations we had experienced in our careers, and how nearly everyone working in nonprofits had similar war stories.

For me, the evidence was at my fingertips. As a trainer who works with nonprofits nationwide, I make it my goal to poke fun at what I call "the crazy": the love/hate relationship between the national office and local chapters; the buffoon boss whom you can't put in front of major donors; the corporate executive who can't believe you work for nonprofits and are actually *smart*; or how hard you have to fight to the death internally to get anything done. Every time I quipped about the circus, the reaction was the same: stunned by my bluntness, eyes would widen, and then broad smiles would appear, followed by laughs of agreement and sighs of relief.

Somebody felt their pain.

It's crazy, I tell you. This nonprofit business is nuts. Yet, at the same time, it's one of the best, most important industries on the planet, comprised of mostly passionate, good-hearted people. We are angels on earth, each trying to do the right thing and, in reality, making a tremendous impact on the world.

Despite its quirks and idiocies, I have been truly blessed to call the nonprofit sector my home for twenty years. I chose to stay, as have millions of my colleagues, because of a deep-seated belief that our work is needed, necessary, and tied to something bigger than ourselves.

Yet, to stay sane and survive (not to mention to learn, grow and re-energize), it's important to step back, look at the absurdity, and have fun with it.

For me, that's when the light bulb came on. The not-for-profit world doesn't need another textbook. We need a laugh! We need to hear the stories of those who came before us, who walked the road, wore out their shoes and endured the road rash. Most importantly, through those wonderful stories, we can learn the tools we need to "manage the crazy."

That's the kind of book I would want to read. That's the kind of book I would want to write.

So I did.

These stories could happen to any one of us (and most likely have). I hope you'll enjoy my innocent jabs at ourselves and our industry, and equally important, I hope you'll see the lessons inherent in each and every story. Take those lessons and put them into practice in the daily work you do.

And when you find yourself tightly wound, all stressed out or banging your head against the wall, open this book and remind yourself that it's all just Nonprofit Nonsense.

"...and now, for our next agenda item!"

MISPERCEPTIONS OF NONPROFIT WORK

I never thought I'd work in nonprofits. After all, who wants to work their butt off and not make any money in life?

It's a common belief about nonprofits: that we're in a small-money, big-dream industry, living on the low end of the economic food chain.

It may be a common thought, but it is *wrong*—and it's one of the *many* misperceptions I've found about the nonprofit industry.

Why the industry owns this second-class stigma is baffling. According to the *Nonprofit Almanac 2012*, the nonprofit sector employs 13.7 million people in the United States or approximately 10 percent of the country's workforce.[1] That means 1 in every 10 Americans works for a nonprofit, more than all who work in the finance industry—including insurance and real estate—combined. Economically, nonprofits drive more than $1.51 trillion in revenue and contribute $804.8 billion worth of output annually to the U.S. economy, making up 5.5 percent of the country's GDP.[2] While it's true that nonprofits, in general, don't lead the pack in compensation, they're not lagging as far behind as most people think. According to the U.S. Bureau of Labor Statistics, nonprofit salaries are roughly comparable to those in for-profit businesses. With nearly 1.6 million IRS-registered nonprofits, the sector is the country's third largest labor force behind retail trade and manufacturing, accounts for 9.2 percent of all the wages and salaries paid, and continues to grow faster—in terms of employees and wages—than business or government.[3]

The truth is you can have a very nice career and make a fine living in the nonprofit sector. It *is* big business.

So why is it treated with such *disdain*?

One reason could be its fragmentation. The industry is comprised of more than 1.6 million *independent, sole and separate* organizations, each trying to build its own boat (and, quite frankly, trying to row it alone).

Most of these organizations are small-to-medium-sized, community-based hospitals, museums, private schools, religious institutions, orchestras, public television, youth groups, radio stations, soup kitchens, and foundations. There is no powerful union, campaign-contributing lobbyists, or stock exchange to represent the industry. Neither the NYSE, NASDAQ nor the S&P 500 tracks nonprofits. There isn't a nonprofit ticker tape constantly running across the bottom of my TV screen, and unless there is a major scandal, the media doesn't cover our restructuring or layoffs, announcements of our new strategic plans, or filings of our IRS Form 990s. While there's a lot to like about our relative obscurity, it's also why the nonprofit sector hasn't been able to throw its weight around as powerfully as it might. It's a ten-pound gorilla wearing a tutu.

Another reason could be found in the term "nonprofit" itself. The word is *nonsense*. Of course there's profit—otherwise, I wouldn't have had a job in fundraising for the past twenty years. It's what you **do** with the profit that delineates the difference between a nonprofit and a for-profit organization.

I once worked with a general counsel who summed it up beautifully. "We are a *not-for-profit*," she explained. "We *should* generate revenue, and be good stewards of those dollars, including being profitable. The end game, however, isn't about distributing dividends to shareholders so that they can buy a Lamborghini. Instead, as a not-for-profit, we reinvest the profits back into achieving the mission."

Here's one more potential culprit: all too often, some of our own staffers forget this "profit versus nonprofit" differential and use the not-for-profit designation as an excuse to be non-professional, non-entrepreneurial, non-businesslike and non-assertive. They distribute ugly yellow fliers, never update the recorded message, allow their website to get woefully out-of-date, forget to call parents of a cancelled youth program, or send out direct mail pieces with typos and grammar errors.

"We're *just* a nonprofit. People don't expect much from us," they exclaim.

I've seen it. A corporate sponsor donates one million dollars and the program staff forgets to put the sponsor's logo on the underwritten brochure. "Oops," they say breezily.

A large group of employees raises a half a million dollars to provide scholarships for kids, but discovers the money had funded adult education classes instead.

"Well, it's still for educational purposes," one staff member justifies.

"Won't they just be pleased we're doing good work with their money?" a program director asks, as she shrugs her shoulders, giving me her oopsy-doodle eyes.

Hmmm, let me think…**No!**

Regardless of size, nonprofits are still businesses. They must run efficiently and professionally to thrive. Members, donors, sponsors, volunteers, supporters all have expectations, which they want met. They *choose* whom to support, and with 1.6 million nonprofits, they can easily take their support elsewhere.

Finally, one of the funniest misperception outsiders have about nonprofits is that internal politics don't exist and that we're all sitting around the water cooler singing *Kumbaya* together.

Au contraire.

Just like for-profit businesses, the nonprofit industry possesses some tough internal politics, particularly in the large federated systems. Negotiations regularly take place over donors, budgets, territory, and power. Which department or chapter gets to claim the donor? Who gets to book the revenue? Which cost center will take the hit for the expense? Why must the national office have its nose in everything? Can't the chapters just follow the rules? What happens when the media misdeeds of one chapter bleed into the territory of another chapter? Why doesn't someone just make a decision?

Nonprofits enjoy all the same highs and lows as corporate America: great bosses vs. nincompoops; stellar vs. lousy cultures; well run machines vs. those held together with duct tape; financial strength vs. brink of dissolution. We endure the same, typical day-in, day-out challenges of any large or small business.

So, you're not going to get rich in a nonprofit job, and we've established that you're going to face most (or all) of the same roll-your-eyes, pain-in-the-tush kinds of problems that plague every business. So why do we stick with it?

Here's what I believe: whatever we may miss in compensation or stock plans, we make up for in valuable life experience—the kind you can't get anywhere else.

Nonprofit work teaches you how to build something out of nothing; to pull yourself up by your bootstraps; to scrap and scrounge; to get things done with little money and fewer resources. You learn to promote without a budget; develop fearlessness in asking for help; discover there are ten ways to creatively accomplish a goal; and master relationship-building skills. Eventually, you can build the Empire State Building out of Popsicle sticks.

If the world ever went to hell in a hand basket, I am pretty sure that the nonprofit professionals would find a way to survive.

I actually began my career in the for-profit world. Out of college, I worked in corporate America, hired to sell hotel rooms for an international hotel chain. "Heads and beds" is what we called it. The training was amazing. The benefits and pay were lucrative. The ladder was tall, and the infrastructure robust. Young and full of enthusiasm, I'd come up with a new way to expedite check-in or a clever new ad slogan. In true corporate style, I was encouraged to write the idea on a quality card and put it in the quality box, and the quality circle would review it at the next meeting (probably next year). They had put me in a box, and for me, boxes are coffins.

Finding my way to the nonprofit world was like a kid walking into a candy shop. When I raised my hand saying, "Hey, I think there is a better way to do that," or, "I think I could make that happen," I was awarded the workload. (For nonprofits, the reality is there's way too much work to be done by too few people with far too few resources, so you get plenty of opportunity to try your hand at things and wear different hats. For folks like me, it can be endlessly thrilling. And exhausting.)

That brings me full-circle, to what clearly is *not* a misperception of nonprofit work: the validation that comes within from knowing you're doing the right thing, and witnessing the results of your hard work. Sometimes success is measured in moving the needle incrementally towards finding a cure or eradicating disease, poverty or hunger—big audacious goals addressing issues that have plagued our planet for centuries.

For others, end results *can* be seen, measured and celebrated every day: a family opens the door to a new home; thousands are served meals during a natural disaster; a child receives a prosthetic leg; a village enjoys safe drinking water without having to walk fifteen miles; a homeless veteran is sheltered; an abused child finds a place of respite; a woman starts her life over with job training; a scholarship gets a teen out of the ghetto; one species avoids extinction; a sick child gets her wish.

When we look back, we see our footprints in the sand and know we've made a difference. It helps us make sense of our lives. It is this *raison d'être* that plants itself deeply in the hearts and souls of nonprofit professionals, and gives us the stamina to endure the nonsense.

"Which hat shall I wear in THIS meeting?"

3

NONPROFIT IS SERIOUS BUSINESS

"Burdens become light when cheerfully borne."

Ovid

Our nonprofit has organized a two-day, all-staff retreat. Everyone is excited because a representative from Southwest Airlines is our keynote guest speaker. He has come to talk with us about innovation, creative branding and customer service. The audience welcomes him with a thunderous applause, and, with his tuneful Texas accent, he begins:

"I was so excited to come here today. I was thinking to myself this is a group of folks who work every day with kids and families, using sports, recreation and fun activities to make the world a better place…I was thinking, man, this is going to be fun!"

He freezes, holding the thought in mid-air. His pregnant pause is noticed.

"Man, y'all are puckered!" he jabs.

Everyone in the room jumps, eyes widen and jaws drop. Within seconds, nervous laughter begins. We squirm uncomfortably in our chairs, experimenting with the new concept of laughing at ourselves. It isn't something we are used to; not something we are good at.

He goes on to tell great stories and make his two main points:

1. **Levity leads to creativity.**

    To alleviate stagnation and drive innovation, people must feel safe to shake things up, break the mold, and try new things. After all, do I really care whether my flight attendant is wearing pantyhose and pumps or preppy shorts and a golf shirt? If suddenly in a situation where you're saving my life by deploying emergency slides and administering oxygen masks, I'd prefer you chuck the heels.

2. Personality gets attention.

To get people's attention in this message-cluttered world, your brand must have personality. Just because you have something serious to convey, doesn't mean you have to seriously bore people to death. Southwest still follows the FAA regulations, but adds a little dash of whimsy along with it.

I've never forgotten that guy, because he put his finger right on the pulse of this industry. Nonprofit is serious business. We are generally cautious, careful and protective of what we have. We are quick to label new ideas as dangerous, take months to build internal consensus, meet to death, and regularly succumb to paralysis by analysis. New ideas are scrutinized, ripped apart and examined from every direction—and that's before the lawyers get a hold of it! Add to it the ridiculously long hours, limited resources, exhausting pace and endless need—it's no surprise that, as an industry, we are tightly wound. **Puckered**.

But can you blame us? People's lives *do* depend on us. We're trying to cure diseases, find a missing child, and ensure people still have drinking water in 20 years. It often *is* life or death work, or at least life-altering work. It takes blood, sweat and tears to build a nonprofit. So, whether we're protecting the robust charitable ship built over the last 100 years, working on a start-up in which we've contributed our own nest egg to create, or a mid-size charity that's about to sustain itself for years to come, we guard our nests like doting mothers, ensuring the health of our reputation, donor trust, tax-exempt status and Charity Navigator rating.

It takes creativity, innovation and energy to work in this business. It takes pride, love and hope. These are all uplifting, spirited attributes that can be powerfully fueled by laughter and wit. We need to let our hair down more often, take our hands off the handlebars, and allow the ride to take us somewhere new. In other words, we need to lighten up.

Start with the following:

Brighten up the offices with lots of natural light and inspiring color. Open up workspaces by removing walls, tall-walled cubicles and obstructions that force people to separate rather than collaborate.

Cheer often. Welcome new staff with a marching band and greet visiting volunteers and donors with cheers. When a staffer leaves, honor that person with a classy, gracious thank you.

Embrace the class clowns. Turn to the one or two staffers who naturally make it their job to instigate fun, add levity to tough situations, and inherently serve as the "go-to" people for comfort, counsel and understanding. These folks are your organization's health-barometers and culture-trendsetters. Ignore them, defuse their energy or stomp on them, and everyone's heart light dims. Celebrate them, feed them and empower them to shine, and everyone's attitude and productivity will rise.

Release the innovative spirit. That's what attracted your staffers to charity-work in the first place: the desire to care, connect and change. Have real brainstorming sessions:

- Hand out crayons, beach balls, playdough and squirt guns.

- Allow people to throw ideas around uninterrupted, without judgment, and encourage others to build off it.

- Schedule innovation days—a day once a month free of meetings for teams to create, think, and develop ideas to continuously improve the business, processes and culture.

- Allow feedback and criticism to not be viewed as threatening, but as caring—caring enough to voice an opinion while also offering a commitment to find a solution or a better way.

- Let staff at all levels champion ideas that get put into practice.

Leaders who feed this spirit build great brands and great success. After all, if your charitable purpose is to positively impact people's lives, isn't it only right to start internally first?

Enlightened leaders and boards encourage associates to safely spread their wings, color outside the lines, and push the envelope to breakthrough. You *can* protect the brand *while* empowering people to soar.

Puckering stagnates growth, internal culture and revenue. So work hard. But play and laugh more along the way. It's good for business and the world.

NOTE TO SELF: Lighten up!

"Would you prefer to be seated in the
non-fun or for-fun section?"

4

THE DAY I DIED

For six months, I'd been negotiating a deal with a local radio station to put $750,000 worth of spots on-air for a three-month period, with an additional $250,000 in cash sponsorships from local businesses. It was to be the cornerstone of our new campaign to raise funds and heighten awareness for the cause.

Senior executives of the station invited the CEO and me to their offices to finalize the deal. Seated at the board table, we each offered our individual introductions. When it came to my CEO's turn, he cleared his throat and these are the words that actually came out:

"Thank you for inviting us today. I saw in your front lobby, hanging on the wall, your corporate mission statement. **I never imagined that a crass organization like this would have a mission statement.** I found that really impressive. Oh, and I'm Joe Joseph, CEO of the XYZ Foundation."

I peered down, searching for the bullet hole in my heart as I visualized my body sliding under the table, never to be resuscitated. The radio executives looked at each other, stunned and clearly wondering, "Who the hell is this guy?" I could almost imagine slowly raising my hand from under the table to confess, "Yes, he's with me. I brought him."

The next person in the introduction sequence opts for the "just pretend it didn't happen" approach. "Umm, I'm Janet Blip. I'm director of sales for the station."

I continue to hold my breath. The next person, looking none too pleased, introduces himself: "Hello, I'm Rob Dobb, the general manager of this *crass* organization."

And I die. A million-dollar deal and six months of cultivation—gone in one sentence. As the adage states, "It takes years to build up trust, and only seconds to destroy it." My second had arrived.

Truly, sometimes the best thing you can do is to call out the elephant in the room, and that's what the radio station manager had done. Mercifully, his staff grabbed the lifeline and began to chuckle. Tension lightened (although I knew no one was going to forget). My CEO just looked confused.

I was lucky that day. The deal still went forward because the idea was bigger than any one of us. I did a lot of tap dancing, downed several antacids and watched as no one really engaged my CEO in any further conversation. His foot-in-mouth didn't derail the objective, but it put a memorable kink in it.

The good news about nonprofit work is, most of the time, companies want to help. They believe in the mission and the organization as a whole. They see the value and return on investment (ROI) that intrigued them in the first place and look at the staff, CEO included, as a complete deck of cards, not just one king or queen. As long as they have trust and confidence in a handful of players, you can often survive a wild-card boss. But not always. If one truly believes leadership starts and trickles down from the top, then it is only a matter of time before these blunders will permanently offend a potential corporate partner or donor and kill the deal.

I survived a series of other comparable episodes with this particular CEO. He told a waiter, "No, I don't touch the stuff" when offered a soft drink while dining with the PepsiCo marketing team. He jabbed the executives from KFC during a lunch at their corporate headquarters, "I caught you pulling the skin back on that chicken!"

I needed to seek relief for my growing ulcer. A colleague once offered me a valuable piece of advice: "Always put a board member between yourself and trouble," she explained. Only a board member can trump a CEO, so I hooked my wagon to the chair of the board's fundraising committee, a smart, articulate businesswoman who intuitively understood my goals. I convinced my CEO that the best way to keep the board engaged was to have her, the committee chair, accompany me whenever a "title" was required. Thankfully, he supported this strategy, and delegated the corporate appearances to us.

My ulcer subsided, and I continue to believe that may have been the most valuable advice I ever received during my nonprofit career.

 NOTE TO SELF: Always put a board member between yourself and trouble.

"I'd like to introduce one of our most ardent supporters, um...
a man who needs no introduction...um, ah...Mister..."

5

MISSION CREEP

"You must choose, but choose wisely, for as the real grail brings eternal life, the false grail brings death."

Ancient Knight Templar
Indiana Jones and The Last Crusade (1989)

Now that I am over forty, this happens to me a lot: I begin walking with vigor to the other end of the house, clearly headed for the kid's bedroom. I arrive, stop, look around, and have absolutely no idea why I'm there. What did I come for? What was my mission? No clue.

Mission creep among nonprofits is the same basic concept. You start moving with force, energy and determination towards a mission, yet you wake up one day and find yourself somewhere else. You wonder, "What the hell am I doing here?"

A common quip within the industry is that we don't know the word "no." We bite off far more than we can chew, aim to please everyone, and try to do too much.

I once held a focus group for moms to explore how the charity could add value to their membership. While, we felt, we did a great job caring for their kids in our after-school programs, perhaps membership would rise if they saw greater value and customer service. We tested a couple of suggestions submitted via member comment cards:

"Would it be helpful if we partnered with a dry cleaner so that you could drop off your laundry with us when you bring your kids to daycare in the morning and have it clean when you return after work?

Would it be nice to have more family picnics so you could get to know the parents of the other kids in the child care program?"

The focus group participants began round-tabling the concepts. After some deliberation, a woman, who had been silent up to that point, held up her hand in the stop position. Her words caused the group to pause.

She said, "Please, just take great care of my child." So simple, and yet so easy to forget.

We know the adage, "You can't be all things to all people." Yet, it's hard for nonprofits to hold the line against mission creep. The additional money, prestige, control and need can be very compelling. But you have to focus. There's too much work to be done in the world, and you simply don't have enough money or resources to do it all. When you succumb to mission creep, eventually, you collapse under the weight of your good intentions.

Choose your mission wisely, and stick to it. It's all good. It's all noble.

But it's not all necessary.

Don't end up in the kid's bedroom wondering how the hell you got there.

MISSION CREEP

"Sure, we can do that. And that..."

6
YOUR MAN ON THE MOON

The U.S.S.R. began the space race by launching Sputnik I in 1957. In April of 1961, Russian Cosmonaut Yuri Gagarin became the first human to visit space; American Astronaut Alan Shepard made the first U.S. space flight one month later in Freedom 7.

On May 25, 1961 during a special address to Congress, U.S. president John F. Kennedy challenged NASA with a bold declaration:

> "I believe that this nation should commit itself to achieving the goal, before this decade is out, of landing a man on the Moon and returning him safely to the Earth."

His speech contained numerous references to the collective commitment and burden. The president challenged us to be all in or all out.

> "I believe we possess all the resources and talents necessary. But the facts of the matter are that we have never made the national decisions or marshaled the national resources required for such leadership. We have never specified long-range goals on an urgent time schedule, or managed our resources and our time so as to insure their fulfillment…In a very real sense, it will not be one man going to the Moon—if we make this judgment affirmatively, it will be an entire nation. For all of us must work to put him there…It is a heavy burden, and there is no sense in agreeing or desiring that the United States take an affirmative position in outer space, unless we are prepared to do the work and bear the burdens to make it successful. If we are not, we should decide today and this year."

Only eight years later, in July of 1969, Neil Armstrong took "one small step for [a] man; one giant leap for mankind." America won the race for space by setting a goal, sticking to the plan, and *asking everyone to make the sacrifices necessary to achieve success.*

Where you focus is where you will go, and teamwork is what will take you there.

Clear vision defines a great leader. No staff or group can exert maximum talent and energy blindly. They need to see the end-goal in order to feel confident that they know where they're headed. This is management's job: clearly articulate the vision, give people the tools and resources to get the job done, and get out of the way.

Great leaders also instill faith in teamwork. Each staff member and volunteer not only comprehends the vision, but believes wholeheartedly that everyone is on the same team, rowing the same direction, and that his/her role is vital and valued. Just as President Kennedy stated so beautifully:

> "In a very real sense, it will not be one man going to the Moon—if we make this judgment affirmatively, it will be an entire nation. For all of us must work to put him there..."

In 1962, three janitors worked at NASA. A reporter decided to interview each one for a story he was writing about President Kennedy's speech. He stopped the first janitor in the hallway and asked him, "What are you doing?" He replied, "I'm mopping this floor." He stopped the second janitor and asked, "What are you doing?" He said, "I'm cleaning the tile." He stopped and asked the third janitor, "What are you doing?" The third janitor responded, "I'm working to put a man on the Moon."

So, here's my question for you: *what do you do?*

Repeatedly, when I ask nonprofit professionals what they do, I uniformly get responses like "I'm in fundraising." Or: "I'm in marketing." "I'm a program director." "I work with at-risk kids." "I work in the HR department of a nonprofit." "I work in accounting."

Really? Is that *really* what you're on this planet to do? Or are you…

…working to eliminate diabetes?

…fixing our education system?

…protecting forests?

…ensuring people don't go hungry?

I have a feeling that, no matter what your job description, you're in this business for reasons much larger than your occupation. When I was with the Make-A-Wish Foundation, I enjoyed overhearing my kids tell their teachers and classmates what their mom did for a living. They'd say, "My mom grants wishes!" From the mouth of babes comes the truth. That was the team I was playing for—that was my man on the Moon.

The movie *Miracle* is about the underdog, 1980 U.S. Olympic Hockey team that won gold. The team was comprised of collegiate All-Stars, each with a vicious sense of rivalry—for each other.

Coach Herb Brooks knew his team was over-matched by the European professional teams, particularly Russia. The only way for his team to have a prayer was to come together as one unit, one team.

Coach Brooks would continuously ask his new players, "Where ya from? Who do you play for?" The respondent would habitually identify his hometown and college team of affiliation. The coach never challenged the response, letting it go. He repeatedly asked this question, and always got the same answer.

After being beaten by the Norwegian national team in a practice game leading up to the Olympics, he forced them to perform excruciating drills, skating the length of the ice—and each line in-between—over and over (to this day, hockey players refer to these drills as "Herbies"). "Send them," the coach ordered,

"Again."

"Again."

"Again."

The drill repeated well into the night, even after the lights in the stadium were turned off. Players were on their knees, exhausted and in pain. Egos and defiance had been stripped away. Finally, Coach Brooks got the response he was looking for.

"Who do you play for?" the coach asked Mike Eruzione (who later went on to score the winning goal in the championship game).

For the first time, the answer was clear: "I play for the United States of America."

Fragmented vision, silos, distrust and fear are toxic to any organization. Unify your team and, like the 1980 Olympic hockey champions, the rest will be history.

What is Your mission?
Can you explain it in 15 seconds?

Staff and volunteers should each be able to describe what your charity does in a 15- to 30- second "elevator speech." (An elevator speech is based on the average time it takes to ride from the ground to the top floor in an elevator.)

Typically it's not appropriate to recite your mission statement, which tends to be a written affirmation that isn't very conversational in nature. Instead, an elevator speech is a chatty, friendly explanation of what your charity does and how it does it. It's the sales pitch for why anyone should care, be impressed, and want to engage. If it takes one, two or three minutes to explain, you've clearly lost your way.

NOTE TO SELF: Where you focus is where you will go, and teamwork is what takes you there.

MANY HANDS MAKE LIGHT WORK

7

PERMANENT CREASE

Throughout my career, I found myself wondering how the heck I ended up in the Nonprofit Olympics. Of course, I never trained for this, and I certainly never had my sights set on gold. I simply signed up to raise money and write press releases for a nonprofit organization. Somehow, some way, I ended up in the fundraising high jump competition, reaching for heights I never imagined.

It typically goes something like this (see if this sounds familiar to you):

> The Boss walks in and says, "We're increasing your fundraising goal this year by 50 percent. We also need to cut your budget by 25 percent. And sorry, remember that admin position you requested? No can do. Maybe next year."

> A sinking feeling overwhelms me. I am stunned, wondering how I'm going to pull this one out of my hat. I find the weight of the world very heavy. Maybe it's time to give up, but I don't.

> Perhaps it's my unwavering desire to win, or an inherited sickness that drives me to prove I can conquer any challenge set before me. I jump, dance, crouch, crawl, roll and dive—whatever it takes to prove my super skills. Somehow I manage to make that new goal.

> You see, they—the bosses—know I'm going to hit that goal; that's why they set it so high. They can smell my Superwoman scent.

> The reward for using my nonprofit Super-powers? Nope, it's not a bonus. Not a bigger office or a heartier expense budget. It's another goal increase.

> "You've got to be kidding!" I say to myself, as I reach into my fishbowl of Tylenol.

That night, I look in the mirror and I see two deep vertical lines running perpendicular to my eyebrows. They didn't used to be there. Now, they've become quite dominant and I don't like them.

The doctor kindly explains to me, "As a person ages, years of making facial expressions, combined with thinning skin, leads to frown lines. Over time, it makes a permanent crease."

My permanent crease comes from making the same facial expression day after day. You know: it's the one you make after hearing yet another ridiculous goal or ludicrous idea, and you say, "Seriously???? Seriously!!!"

Most nonprofit folks I know use the word "seriously" ten times a day, minimum. It's the only natural response besides, "Are you frickin' kidding?"

I examine the deep crevices again, and wonder if Botox would fix it. Or a well-deserved vacation. Unfortunately, I know exactly what the cure is: more staff, more money and more resources.

You know that's not going to happen.

I fuss with the scowl lines—contemplating Botox yet again.

 NOTE TO SELF: The higher you jump, the higher you jump.

YEAR-END REVIEW

8

LOCAL VERSUS NATIONAL

Here's a newsflash: a massive love/hate relationship typically exists between the national office and local chapters of most nonprofits. I know, you're shocked.

I've worked and consulted for many top nonprofits in America. It doesn't matter where you go, the national/local headbutting is commonplace. The national office is often the ivory tower: the 10,000-foot view, protector of all things sacred, the vast depository for best practices, the loudspeaker for the brand, and the keeper of the almighty charter. The local offices or chapters are in the trenches, where the programs and services live, day-in and day-out, where folks make parachutes out of pillow cases, lemonade out of lemons, and deliver the goods by a mule, if need be. Both are earnestly trying to do the right thing. Both are vitally important and have their role.

When done right, it becomes a strategic, divide and conquer engine. National takes care of the global, umbrella stuff. It cares for the collective brand, manages the repetitive processes, collects and shares data, facts and information across the board. The chapters focus on the specific implementation and delivery of the programs, the customization according to demographics and demands of the community, and the one-on-one, grassroots engagement.

I've had the pleasure of working in both camps and seeing the world through both lenses. Neither is better or worse, right or wrong. They're just different vantage points.

> It's my first week on staff at the national office. I'm walking the halls, meeting people, and discovering file drawers and shelves filled with tools and resources I never knew existed.

> "Damn," I say to myself, "I would have loved to use this with my donors. If I'd known all that was hidden away up here, my life would have been so much easier!"

My watch tells me it's time for the meeting on the newly announced signature campaign. People are chatting excitedly as I enter the room. They like how the campaign is shaping up, and are convinced it will rival the ones in the marketplace generating eight-figure revenue.

Amidst their enthusiasm, I imagine the dialogue amongst my friends back at the local chapter: "A signature campaign? They tried that eight years ago and it was a total flop. So what are they proposing this time? Are they expecting us to coordinate events? Pitch media? Pull off a bunch of miracles? They better have something in it for us this time, and send over some money and bodies to make it all happen. They think we have nothing else to do but implement their ideas. I don't remember them asking us for our ideas. Seriously, what's in this for us? I think all the money stays at national anyways. I haven't seen anything telling us what the goals of this campaign are! And who came up with that stupid logo? It's stupid, don't you agree! Who hired these guys?"

I shake off the daydreaming, and focus attention on the meeting. Over the course of the next two hours, I'm impressed with the thoughtfulness and intelligence of the conversation. They've prepared an entire road show of communiqués, one-sheets, web pages, campaign materials-in-a-box, scheduled speeches at workshops and trainings, and even more plans. It seems thorough and thoughtful. But then I remember where I came from, and how no one ever really had time to sit and digest these materials—and how even with this detailed level of planning, most chapter folks will still have no idea what this thing is about.

My thoughts are interrupted when I'm asked, "What do you think? How will chapters respond?"

I hesitate. I consider the ramifications of being labeled the new Debbie Downer if I share how chapters think about stuff like this…but my role isn't to blow smoke at them either. "Well, I'm not sure if the local chapters are as excited about this as you are." All eyes affix on me.

"I think we need to be really clear, in any and all communications, in terms of **what's in it for them**. What do we expect them to do? Who will pay for it and who will fund the labor? Where will the money raised go? What are the measurable goals for the national office, for the local chapters, and how will we evaluate success? Truth is, they'll never know or appreciate how much research, thought or work goes into crafting all this. You've done an amazing job. But if they can't clearly find the answers to these questions, they'll read no further. You have to lead with this conversation right at the start every time, and repetition will be key. The rest is interesting and important, but they'll hear it as 'blah, blah, blah' if you haven't answered the core questions first."

As I try to fall asleep that night, I feel good about my contribution. Perhaps I shortened the gap between national and the chapters just a tad today, at least in terms of this campaign. Regardless, I couldn't help but be in awe. The other side isn't the enemy. They're trying just as hard. I used to think the national staff was a bunch of buffoons; that they just didn't get it. Now I see that they're actually trying.

As I drift off, I wonder how long before I'm so deep into the national office workload that my chapter eyes will start to fail me. I give myself two months and fall asleep.

Where does this love/hate relationship stem from?

Likely, it comes from the same place that generates distrust among different peoples, cultures and countries: we don't know each other. Our ignorance of the other's reality is what keeps us from appreciating and respecting the nuances.

And it can make you nuts.

Karen sits in her cubicle, plowing through the endless stream of emails (two hundred a day, on average). Ping. Email alerts her that the weekly national e-newsletter has arrived. She scrolls. Same old, same old: the website will be down for maintenance; national finally filled the job that has been vacant for five months; just secured a national corporate sponsor. Karen gives this last item a closer look. The article reads, "We are happy to announce a national relationship with a quick-serve restaurant which will generate $500,000 for the organization." They're celebrating. Karen sits up in her chair, now worried. She quickly composes an email asking how the new national relationship might affect the cause marketing deal she has in the works with a different quick-serve restaurant with eight locations in her state. It's worth $50,000 to the chapter, a big deal in this neck of the woods.

Ping. "Sorry, our new contract includes an exclusivity clause and prohibits us from doing cause marketing deals with competitors."

Bye, bye to that prospect. Karen's blood boils.

Cindy stands at the end of her driveway, sorting the bills and junk mail just retrieved from the mailbox. Her neighbor approaches and asks, "What's the date of the upcoming gala? I'd really like to attend this year." Cindy tries to disguise her blank stare while thinking, "Huh, what gala?" She quickly realizes the neighbor is referring to the local chapter's gala.

She thinks, "Crap, I have no idea. Just because I work *at* the national office in Denver doesn't mean I know what's happening *in* Denver."

"Uh, I'll have to double check and call you," Cindy promises her neighbor.

Cindy goes inside the house, beating herself up for being so disconnected. She knows this is precisely what makes chapters hate the national office, appearing clueless or disinterested in what's happening locally.

"I *do* care," she rationalizes, "I'm just overwhelmed fighting my own fires that I don't have time to even think." She vows to pay better attention while she makes a note to follow up with her neighbor.

The phone rings. It's a chapter, marketing director asking if she can get permission to do a cause marketing deal in her three-state territory with a fitness center operating 15 locations. They're pushing the latest craze in exercise: pole-dancing. She explains they'll donate 30 percent of all membership fees to our children's charity for anyone who signs up during the month. They are targeting women between the ages of 21-45, and think it will help make the exercise look more wholesome by aligning with us.

I imagine the ad. The visuals don't work for a children's charity. I think of the conversation I'd have to have with senior leadership and legal. I wince at that thought. The image appears in my mind of the laughter following me out the door of our general counsel's office. I choose my words carefully, and explain to the marketing director that I don't think this is a good idea.

There's a long, pregnant pause on the other end. Cautiously she resumes, carefully selecting her words.

"Well, it seems that one of my staff didn't understand our protocol, and kind of gave the fitness center the impression that it would be okay to move ahead. So, they've already released a radio ad in the market, and I'm just finding out about this now." She adds, "And a bigger problem is that the radio ad spills over into another chapter's market, and they don't know anything about this yet…" She pauses. "How should we handle this?"

I lay my head on my desk while still holding the phone. So much for the To Do List I thought I'd conquer today. I now have a whole new set of tasks.

This push/pull between national and the chapters is common, yet you have the power to create an uncommon response. Instead of pushing it aside or chalking it up as inevitable, use the national-local tension as a source of continuous improvement. Strive to reduce it by standing regularly in each other's shoes, actively seeking, listening and responding to constructive criticism, inviting representatives from "the other side" to serve as translators by reviewing and approving communiqués before release, hosting focus groups, polling and surveys that identify weaknesses…and then do something about it. Offer internships, sabbaticals or shadowing-opportunities. Ensure colleagues from both camps network, build relationships, and interact continuously.

Keeping the friction at bay is everyone's responsibility.

NOTE TO SELF: The world looks different depending on the shoes you wear.

9

BADGE OF COURAGE

"Courage doesn't always roar. Sometimes courage is the quiet voice at the end of the day saying; I will try again tomorrow."

Mary Anne Radmacher

I had heard that working for nonprofit sometimes meant you got shit on all over. But I didn't expect it literally.

My office was in the building that also housed the residence tower. Directly above my office was the men's bathroom. The residents living there became disgruntled when the branch executive turned off the air conditioning in order to make budget that month. It was Phoenix in the summer—a toasty 115 degrees.

My intern and I were working, our hair pulled up in ponytails on top of our heads attempting to cool our necks, when it started to rain in our office. It took a few minutes for us to connect the dots: the water was coming not from a broken pipe or leaky roof—it was from flooding. Turns out an angry resident wanted payback for the heat to come in the form of stuffing towels into the toilets, after using them, and letting the waste wash away his loathing.

Down came the brown rain.

My desk, papers and chair were soaked. We ran. I seriously contemplated never going back. Can you blame me?

While someone mopped it up, I knew they hadn't sanitized it. I thought, "I'm not catching some disease over this job!" My boss didn't care.

To protect my intern and myself, I threw around the loose threat of calling the health department until the real cleaning crew arrived.

Years later, this became one of my favorite personal war stories—my own badge of courage, so to speak, earned in the diligent fight to do good in the world.

Everyone in nonprofit has at least one or two of these war stories. Some have many. They are our moments of valor, the instances when we withstand great trial and tribulation—all in the name of sticking up for the underdog. We wonder why we put up with it, yet we choose to push through, endure and survive.

It's because we know what we do matters, and that walking away is not an option.

 NOTE TO SELF: Never office below a bathroom.

"You'll be working 60-hour weeks with no bonus, commissions or stock options...The benefits aren't great, but you'll certainly be making the world a better place!"

10

DO WE REALLY NEED ANOTHER 501(C)(3)?

Let's address the elephant in the room: do we really need another 501(c)(3) in America?

Currently, there are approximately 1.6 million nonprofits registered with the IRS. That's about 1 nonprofit for every 175 Americans. In 2000 the IRS counted a total of 688,600 public charities classified under Section 501(c)(3), the types of organizations to which donors can make tax-deductible donations. Today there are close to 1 million, an astonishing increase of 42.3 percent. Of all public charities, 63 percent were founded in the past 20 years.[4]

I understand the passion folks have to build something from scratch, something they can manage and control. I also understand the appeal of launching a crusade in the name of a loved one, and appreciate the tax advantages for the wealthy and corporations in having their own foundation. Yet at some point, we need to stop recreating and start reinforcing.

Every time a new 501(c)(3) is born, money and energy goes into creating infrastructure, back-end systems and capacity. Each needs an accounting office, legal assistance, HR, payroll, volunteer coordinators, et cetera. Rather than allowing Noah to finish his mission, we spend our resources building another Ark.

Instead of investing in an entirely new build, explore ways to contribute your passion and dedication to a 501(c)(3) that already exists. Imagine the potential impact of several non-competitive but complementary nonprofits, each with its own expertise, uniting around a common cause. For example, unite a literacy advocacy group, a nonprofit for dyslexic children, a nonprofit that contributes books to school libraries, and the librarian association in a bundled collaboration with a corporate sponsor, each putting its assets and expertise on the table…That could make an incredible dent. Now imagine if they all took part in a cooperative that handles their accounting, HR and payroll, and are housed in a centralized office building each sharing training space, conference rooms, a receptionist, copiers, technology and bulk purchasing. That equates to a lot of saved time and energy put to better use furthering the mission.

I jumped for joy when Warren Buffet announced in 2010 that he would give away 85 percent of his wealth to five existing foundations, with the majority ($30 billion) going to the world's largest philanthropic organization, the Bill & Melinda Gates Foundation. Not only did Buffet challenge extremely rich people to vastly distribute their wealth while alive so they can witness and champion the impact, he sent the powerful message to strengthen that, which already exists.

Bill Gates responded, saying that the funding would allow the foundation to "both deepen and accelerate" its work. That's the understatement of the century.[5]

Nonprofit professionals understand that we have limited time and resources, and that the energy that goes into achieving the mission takes great blood, sweat and tears. We need to focus, do what we do best, and collaborate to ensure stuff gets done. Nonprofit folks know this. Want this. Believe this.

But it has yet to happen in a meaningful way. Some great nonprofit-to-nonprofit alliances do exist. They predominately occur in the program delivery space: relief organizations coordinating in a crisis; hunger organizations teaming with schools to feed kids living in poverty; cancer organizations partnering with nonprofit health and wellness groups to sponsor smoking cessation programs. But they're the exception, not the norm.

It's not that we lack the answers. Not even that we, as a people and planet, lack the resources. **We lack the coordination.**

Public schools are an instructive example. The U.S. education system, as a whole, is failing. I live in Arizona, which always ranks 47th or 48th in the nation for per-pupil spending on education.[6] Pathetic. I serve on my school's PTO, and continuously bury my head in my hands when listening to the discussions of how teachers are rationing copy paper; how we must solicit parents for donations of glue sticks, scissors and paper; and how my kids' classroom doesn't have enough dictionaries for the students. I live in Scottsdale, Arizona (in other words, not a poverty-stricken town). Yet our PTO acts alone. It might call another school to share ideas of successful fundraisers now and then. It might log onto the national PTO or PTA website to get some ideas or tap resources—but probably not. By and large, hardworking, caring parents are doing it on their own. Over and over again. School by school. District by district. State by state. Bless the progress and results local

PTAs/PTOs are able to achieve each school year—for that we should be so grateful. But be real. How much momentum comes from working this way? How much further could they go with more bundled resources and collaboration?

While serving on a panel at an American Marketing Association Nonprofit Marketing conference, I made one simple statement: my belief that the secret weapon for the future will be our ability to collaborate. "The day we work smarter, not harder; pool resources and share infrastructure; team up to provide complementary solutions, and synergistically co-exist; this will be the day that we eradicate the issues of our day."

I didn't realize it was such a provocative statement until the room burst out in applause, and I received a standing ovation. It seemed that, for a moment, we were united in our exhaustion.

Let's be united in more than just our exhaustion. Before starting a sole and separate 501(c)(3), look first to collaborate. Ensure your blood, sweat and tears predominately contribute to your mission, not simply your workload.

NOTE TO SELF: Hook your wagon to others; it lightens your load.

THE FLOOD

"...one million three, one million four..."

II

THE TRUTH LIES WITHIN

Here is a sad truth: my job today is to say what you've been saying all along. As a consultant, I make a living helping fundraising and marketing executives (who are extraordinarily talented and know exactly what they're doing) convince their own senior leaders that they know what they're doing. All too often, I repeat the same words and reinforce the same strategy that the in-house expert has been putting forth for weeks or months. Yet for some reason, my fresh voice gets through and the CEO, board or senior leadership finally hears the truth.

Why is it we pay thousands of dollars recruiting, training and indoctrinating the best candidates, and then after a while, we treat them like another talking head? Many of us have had that experience—you were a genius when they hired you, but after the honeymoon is over, you're an idiot.

> I'm attending the third meeting with senior management to discuss the organization's declining membership numbers. They are set on hiring a blue-chip marketing firm, prepared to spend tens of thousands of dollars running promotions to increase membership enrollment.
>
> As head of communications, I feel it's my job to not only ensure the external marketing messages are both right and compelling, but that the brand promise is genuine and authentic. The organization's retention rate has been plummeting, and is now at an all-time low. Continuously, I've suggested business logic that it costs more to acquire a new member than to keep an existing member; that we should be conducting exit interviews; that we need to address the heart of the matter: why are members leaving?
>
> "It is ineffective to spend money to drive people in the front door, if we're only going to blow them out the back door. We need to spend resources both on steadily attracting new members, while also cultivating and retaining our existing ones."

I'd been with the organization six years, so I might as well be yelling into the wind. They don't hear me. I'm wallpaper. So for the fourth meeting, I scrape together a couple thousand dollars from my budget to hire an outside consultant to join me. She shares the same information I've been sharing the past three meetings. Luckily, they hear her and allow me to allocate a portion of the budget to implement exit interviews, staff training and funding for retention improvement strategies.

The truth is: often the solutions can be found within.

My consulting firm is retained to help a nonprofit CMO write a marketing strategy for the organization. He wants fresh, creative and powerful ideas. The consultants start by interviewing the in-house team, including three senior managers of digital marketing, brand communications and media relations.

We are taken aback and impressed by the ideas and energy bursting to get out of these stifled leaders. They have the answers, if you lay your ego at the door and listen.

The recommendation is obvious: the CMO needs to start empowering and listening to these three smart and talented individuals. Of course, consultants can't charge $20,000 to say that—we need to be the producers of all things smart—so we listen, package and regurgitate much of the in-house brilliance, adding some splash of our own.

It's amazing what happens when staff is empowered to create solutions. I've seen staff produce miraculous results on top of their daily duties simply because they're so exhilarated to be asked and to own the solution. Innovation-within is "a very simple concept based on the premise that those closest to the work know it best. When the ideas of those people, irrespective of their functions and job titles, are solicited and turned immediately into action, an unstoppable wave of creativity, energy and productivity is unleashed throughout the organization."[7]

Yet, as managers, we are often afraid to unleash their power. We fear:

1. they might take their eye off the ball and not get their "real job" done;

2. we might not like what they come up with;

3. we seek the protective shield of a big name agency to hide behind. Should the strategy go south, you can deflect the blame, explaining you hired the best, but they blew it.

I find that the third excuse is the biggest reason people hire consultants. Instead, I argue, you should retain a coach to facilitate the process rather than a consultant to do the job for you. A coach's role is to serve as a sounding board, helping staff make ideas bigger, better, brighter. Coaches help staff extrapolate their ingenuity, push boundaries, set priorities, avoid common pitfalls and stay on task. They teach you to fish; they don't fish for you. As a result, those who know your mission, brand, internal politics and capabilities better than anyone birth the solutions from within. It's the best insurance that whatever gets recommended will get implemented.

Google uses a policy called Innovation Time Off, where Google engineers are encouraged to spend 20 percent of their work time on projects that interest them. In March 2011, consulting firm Universum announced that Google ranks **first** on the list of ideal employers chosen by nearly 25 percent from more than 10,000 young professionals asked.[8] In 2013, *Fortune* magazine ranked Google as **number one** on its *100 Best Companies To Work For* list.[9]

Most of us would give our right arm to have even two hours a month to solely think! Instead, we're too busy rushing to meetings, smoothing feathers of bent colleagues, or dodging the bullets of our inbox. Our lives are mostly reactive—not because we don't know better, but because we can't get out of the fire.

While I am a committed proponent of employee empowerment and innovation within, I learned another valuable lesson the hard way. Remember building sandcastles on the beach, and undoubtedly some notorious brat would come along, kick the moat's embankment, forcing the sides to cave in? You hated that kid. Staff empowerment teams are like sandcastles. They must be protected.

> I've been on the job two weeks. Three internal processes clearly aren't working: (1) membership is flat; (2) we have three different databases, none of which talk to the other; and (3) new staff aren't being properly trained. I'm responsible for membership marketing, so I ask the CEO if I could lead an employee-innovation group that would devise solutions for our challenges. He agrees we need to fix these issues, and encourages me to go forth.

> Staff break into three teams, one around each issue, and work diligently for two months. They analyze the problem, research theories and data, articulate and test solutions. Alas, three strategies are brought forth with great pride and enthusiasm. It comes the time to implement the ideas, but the CEO doesn't think it will work and orders me to bury the plan. To make matters worse, he wouldn't provide any specific details or engage in salvaging anything.

There's nothing worse that rallying staff to build a castle, only to have senior leadership crush the walls. Needless to say their anger and resentment was harsh. The backlash of total disengagement thereafter was brutal. Imagine a trapeze artist in mid-air, reaching and grasping the new bar while refusing to let go of the first. What would happen? He'd tear right down the middle.

And so will your organization if you don't have the support to let go.

This experience taught me a valuable lesson: empowerment starts and stops with the CEO. You can say what you want and dress up a bunch of vice president cheerleaders to rally the troops—but in the end, the CEO is the litmus test. If he/she isn't clearly respectful, appreciative and transparent with the staff, they'll never stick their necks out again. Once you've been to the guillotine, you're never going back.

I also learned that a "go ahead" is not necessarily a commitment to back you. Then, I was young and naive. I assumed his approval to go forth meant he was supportive with the process of solving the programs we'd all recognized were ailing the organization. In his mind, however, he'd given me approval to take them through the process, but not his agreement to adopt their recommendations. It wasn't until after the exercise that I recognized he never intended to even consider it. Had I probed with more questions, fully assesses his management style, analyzed his patterns, I would have known never to take the journey with him at the helm.

Employee empowerment is the hallmark of a stellar organization, yet it is unconditionally dependent upon the steadfast leadership of the CEO. Period. Without his/her total commitment to honor and implement ideas generated from the bottom up—don't go down that road.

THE MARGINALIZED EXPERT

12

WALK THE TALK

*"We need to find the courage to say no to the things and people
that are not serving us if we want to rediscover ourselves
and live our lives with authenticity."*

Barbara De Angelis

To quickly ascertain the authenticity of an organization, simply peek at its employee trainings, conferences, board retreats and all-staff meetings. Gotta love the health organization with employees who devour the morning coffee and cinnamon rolls, followed by the deli express lunch, potato chips, sodas and chocolate chip cookies; or the environmental group spending the day sucking down 8-oz bottled waters, scribbling on flip-chart paper, and everyone jumping in their individual cars to drive home; or the afterschool child care providers who host a donor appreciation reception, but provide no child care services for attendees.

Does your organization *walk its talk*?

Is your mission to build healthy kids? If so, how are the children of your own employees doing? What's your policy for parents who can't come into work due to a sick kid? Can they work remotely or are they docked a day's pay because they have to stay home? What's your employee benefit policy for family members?

Is your mission to eradicate cancer? Do you allow smoking in the building? Are your employees so stressed out that negative toxins are overwhelming their bodies? Is your office LEED-certified? Is the workload so heavy that folks only have time for a fast-food lunch?

Is your mission as a parent/teacher organization to benefit the students at your neighborhood school? If so, have you surveyed the kids recently about what's important to *them*? Or do you only ask the adults?

Does a student representative have a voice on your board? Are their bare necessities met with clean, stocked bathrooms and cold, potable drinking water from clean, accessible water fountains (typically two leading concerns among students themselves)? Do they have ample supplies, manipulatives, books and resources in the classroom or are you busy solely planning the next carnival?

Is your mission to help children learn to read? What do you do to help employees encourage the children and grandchildren in their lives to read? Do you offer scholarships or financial assistance to employees who need tutors to assist their children with lagging reading skills or dyslexia? For recognition gifts, do you send donors plaques and fruit baskets…or *book baskets*?

Walking the talk internally matters. Don't think your internal HR policy doesn't have a way of finding itself into the viral conversation among friends.

> I fly into the town of a global children's charity with my 10-year-old daughter. I am there on leisure travel, but want to stop in and visit with a comrade of mine. No big deal, right? My daughter will just sit quietly and read a book while we chat.
>
> It turns out to be a very big deal.
>
> My friend apologetically explains, "No. Sorry. We're not allowed to have any children in the building. A manager brought her kid to work one day when the babysitter no-showed and some folks had a fit. They didn't want it to get out of control with people thinking they could bring their kid to work if they don't have child care, so they made the announcement 'no kids allowed.' "

This, from a global children's charity with the word *child* in its name?! Even at the corporate headquarters of PetSmart, employees are encouraged to bring their pets to work on Fridays.

The word-of-mouth bitch session this HR rule evoked among the staff to their families, friends and acquaintances was widespread. It isn't so much that anyone even wanted to bring a kid to work, it was just the insult of the proclamation and prohibition. I understand the rationale, but admittedly side with the employees. The incongruence with organizational values is staggering. Really? A ban on children at a children's charity? Nonsense.

Authenticity is on the rise in America. Whistleblowers are starting to call out the hypocrites, and consumers are using social media to point out inconsistencies. Neither nonprofit nor for-profit brands can hide. The power and might is no longer in the pen, but in the keyboard.

Today anyone with a web connection can voice an opinion, start a conversation worldwide, and hold brands accountable. A consumer living in Canada can share his personal story about how United Airlines breaks guitars with twelve million of his closest friends (www.youtube/unitedbreaksguitars). In case you haven't seen the video, here's the scoop: a musician watched, from his seat on the plane, as baggage handlers tossed his guitar and broke it. When the airline failed to respond to his multiple contacts, he put his musical talent to work, wrote and recorded a hilarious song and posted a YouTube video to make sure his point was heard. *The Times* newspaper reported that within four days of the video being posted online, United Airline's stock price fell 10 percent, costing stockholders about $180 million in value.[10]

In 2012, Susan G. Komen for the Cure, experienced this truth firsthand when it sought to withdraw funding from Planned Parenthood and a flurry of backlash ignited via the web.[11]

Public pressure forced the pink ribbon charity to reverse its decision.

Additionally, the scrutiny of corporate/cause alliances is mounting as consumers grow accustomed and savvy to cause marketing.

Recently, consumers went ape over Susan G. Komen for the Cure's alliance with KFC. Even though the organization understandably defended its actions, stating its goal is to educate and engage the maximum number of people in the cause, many consumers just hated the juxtaposition of "for the cure" with pink buckets of fried (actually, grilled) chicken. They didn't see the brands as complementary, so consumers squawked and put a great deal of heat on the alliance.

It's challenging for nonprofits to decide which companies to align with in cause marketing ventures because it's not simply a decision whether or not to accept the money. It's the lure of being able to reach and educate mass audiences, attract new constituents, build the brand, and generate resources. It's not always a black and white decision. It's an agonizing grey zone with an invisible line that you don't want to cross. I sum it up as this: If my mother is walking down a store aisle and sees the messaging, and immediately cocks her head thinking "Huh? That's odd!"—then you shouldn't do the deal.

Brand alignment is a gut reaction based on society's current beliefs behind brands. La-Z-Boy should not sponsor the World's Largest Run. Phillip Morris shouldn't sponsor a kids' wellness program. Dow Chemical can't sponsor your Earth Day. And Spencer's Gifts shouldn't sponsor your local Scouts. You can argue, justify, defend, explain all you want, but if it doesn't intuitively make sense, the public won't buy it.

Finally, corporate social responsibility—the buzzword of the new millennium as consumers now expect companies to play an active role in making the world a better place—is being more carefully examined by consumers for authenticity. If the Earth is deteriorating, companies must demonstrate their role in preserving it and cleaning it up. If human labor is to be respected, companies must show they are not using and abusing child labor, running sweatshops, or unfairly treating workers. If a company strips resources from a country or community to make its products, it has to invest in replenishing the supply. The products a company makes should be considerate of the environment in its packaging as well as its disposal.

Luckily, 300 companies are now members of Business for Social Responsibility (BSR). The Clinton Global Initiative (CGI) has more than 2,000 members from the realms of government, private industry and nonprofit organizations. Many companies are investing significant resources thinking seriously about sustainability, their carbon footprint, what natural materials they use up in production, and how to dispose of waste. Whatever the social issue, business now bears a heavy burden: it must be constantly ready to explain its position, defend its actions, and prove its authenticity. Transparency is key.

Hypocrisy can't survive. Soon enough, no one will get away with a measly third-of-a-cent of some consumer product purchase benefiting charity or a company saying it's committed to water conservation in TV ads while doing nothing to reduce water use in its manufacturing. No longer can a nonprofit horde abundant reserve funds and not distribute the money to advance the mission. No longer will Charity Navigator's single-star charities be able to compete.

NOTE TO SELF: No longer can you say one thing and do another.

HIPPO-CRITS: LEADERS IN HEALTH INITIATIVES

13

LEGAL WOES AND NOES

I've often heard the legal department referred to as "the place where dreams go to die."

I'm a marketer. It's a lawyer's job to curb my enthusiasm, ensure my out-of-the-box, push the envelope thinking doesn't send us over the cliff. They've got their job to do, and I've got mine. We're on the same team, but we often feel juxtaposed. Why is it the general counsel's office gives me flashbacks to grade school, sitting in the principal's office, feeling vulnerable, helpless, and five seconds away from having my mother called?

I've officially earned my honorary law degree. Not because I went to law school, but because I have spent most of my twenty year career visiting the legal department and learning more than I ever wanted to know about nonprofit, promotional law and accounting, unrelated business income tax (UBIT), commercial co-venture registration (CCV), qualified sponsorship payments, substantial return benefit, charitable solicitation registration, variance power, easy-out clauses, indemnification, disclosure language, licensing of the Marks…(Are you snoring yet?).

When legal folks talk, most people's eyes roll back. They're speaking a foreign language, as are their cousins in IT. As with many foreign languages, the meaning of a word can change simply by adjusting the tone or one letter. So it is with lawyers.

"Can I cross the road?"

"No."

"Can I cross the driveway?"

"No."

"Can I cross the sidewalk?"

"Yes."

"Why the sidewalk?"

"Less liability."

"Gotcha."

I shake my head, wondering why he didn't just suggest that I cross the sidewalk instead of the road when I first asked. I'm trying to get somewhere. Help me figure out how to get there.

Most lawyers don't offer up alternatives. I'm convinced law school trains them this way. After all, in a court of law when asked, "Did a man in a red and white hat attack you?" The answer is simply "No." It's not "No, he wore a red and blue hat." It's "no"—period—because when a portion of the statement is inaccurate, the *entire* statement is thereby negated. They learn to answer the question *asked*. No more, no less. Don't elaborate.

"Can we do a contest?"

"No."

"Can we do a sweepstakes?"

"Yes."

Go figure. Sweepstakes, contest—whatever. To me, they're basically the same, and either will accomplish my marketing goal. But to a lawyer, it's two *totally different* legal questions. Yet, if I didn't swap words and ask again, the campaign may have been thwarted. This is why many in corporate relations quip that legal is the department of sales suppression.

I can understand it may be unethical for an attorney to brainstorm loopholes or sneaky ways to circumvent the system—but offering up legal counsel on *how* to word, structure or position something so that it *does work* <u>should</u> be the role of a general counsel.

Think about it this way: if a surgical resident asks the lead surgeon, "I cut this artery, right?" and receives the response of "no" and the resident clearly doesn't know which artery to cut…how long would you let the patient lie on the table waiting for the resident to come up with the right question? Pretty soon you'd use the teaching moment to teach the correct procedure.

Most employees don't know the right questions to ask, are unfamiliar with possible variations, or are simply using layman's terms. Certainly, most aren't assertive enough to persistently drill the general counsel with alternatives until a "yes" is achieved. Attorneys are intimidating. They're the scary legal people who always win an argument, and definitely have more clout with the CEO than you do. Few people want to take 'em on…so they accept the "no" as defeat of the idea. And that's when dreams die.

Learning how lawyers think has helped me be successful and enjoy camaraderie with legal teams throughout my career. Positive persistence is not an effort to wear 'em down or bug them until they cave. (Attorneys don't cave.) Instead, it's realizing that *I am the one* who must offer alternative language, different structures, various scenarios until I achieve my goal while still protecting the organization.

When you uncover what works for legal, you've established precedent. Make a "note to self" and apply it next time to take the easy route.

NOTE TO SELF: Know that "no" doesn't always mean "no";
it means you can't do it THAT way.

"I am the Great and Powerful Attorney!
I will grant you approval once I receive approval to approve..."

14

THE MISPLACED BOARD MEMBER

Why do retired board members think they can do your job blindfolded?

Nothing adds more to the nonsense than a misplaced board member or donor who:

1. micromanages and sticks his/her influence into operational staff decisions;

2. thinks he/she can do everyone's job brainlessly;

3. views the staff as his/her personal slaves;

4. serves as an interim when job vacancies arise;

5. dangles his/her philanthropic donations over the staff's head with every thought, request, idea or whimper.

The board has the fiduciary responsibility to monitor and manage the overall goals and policies of the organization, not to pick out paint colors. The board is responsible for hiring and supervising the CEO and offering direction on budget and finance. The board is NOT responsible for the daily operation of the business.

Who hasn't experienced this kind of scenario?

> Ralph is a board member with lots of wealthy friends. He's retired, having made his money in real estate. He's pledged $1,000,000 over 10 years to the organization, loves the mission and volunteers a tremendous amount of his time. In fact, he seems to wake up daily with new ideas to drive press coverage and potential donations for the charity. He has the vice president of financial development, the CEO and the head of marketing on speed-dial. Today, Ralph sees a TV news piece about a global organization announcing it will redirect all its philanthropic support to one cause: world hunger. He jumps on the phone, calling the

vice president of development. When the assistant answers, he announces himself and directs her to track down the boss.

"Tell him I'm calling, and that it's extremely important."

"Hello, Ralph. How are you?" answers the VP of development.

"I'm great," he replies. "Say, I was just watching the news about XYZ Corporation getting behind the hunger issue. Here's what we should do. Get me a pitch deck, and I'll call Sam who can call George and get us a meeting. Have research get a hold of the company's annual report, a list of its board of directors, and all the charities it has supported in the last 10 years. Have the stuff to me end of day tomorrow, and I'll make the call. Let's get some of that money!"

He goes on.

"By the way, yesterday I shared with Lisa in marketing how I thought WKRP would be an amazing media partner. I told her to call the station manager and line up a meeting for us to discuss a potential alliance. I haven't heard back from her. Do you know if she's done that yet or not? If not, can you transfer me?"

In isolation, this single phone call could be a welcomed, helpful lead. But when replicated weekly (or worse, daily), bearing little to no positive results, the staff learns to dread the calls.

Throughout this book, I discuss the importance of working *smarter* and not *harder*. Every nonprofit wants and needs engaged board members, donors and volunteers. They depend upon their support, liaisons, networks and enthusiasm. The staff, itself, is trying to be strategic and efficient in its efforts and workload. Getting spun around by an overzealous volunteer or donor can undo all that hard work. It becomes a tail wagging the dog.

A better outcome to this scenario would have been for the board member to send an FYI email or phone call to the VP of development letting him know about the news story. He could have included information about any contacts or ideas of how to open the door with prospective companies, and offered to help pitch. Put the ball in the VP's court.

To board members out there, remember: don't assign workload and deadlines, pull people out of meetings, order staff to conduct research, prepare reports or write proposals because you think it is good idea. When you do, you're out-of-bounds.

THE MISPLACED BOARD MEMBER

15

NONPROFIT IT

Nonprofit IT. There's an oxymoron. We all love to make fun of our information technology (IT) department—it's akin to jokes about lawyers. Then the day comes when they save your butt, and suddenly a whole new level of appreciation forms.

We can't live in the world anymore without dealing with IT. Nonprofits are no exception. We must store our data, keep our history, track our financials and interact with our colleagues, donors, supporters and critics. We're all tangled in the worldwide web, and now we're playing in the cloud. It's only getting more intense.

Many nonprofits are all over this trend, investing heavily in IT, building robust, integrated databases, customizing consumer-driven content and digital engagement, leveraging social media, ensuring convenient online registration and user-friendly websites, and gathering richly-sourced consumer data that provides insight and knowledge about the likes and preferences of each supporter. Sadly, too many others are still dragging their heels, resisting the inevitable. For them, the IT department is still predominately charged with putting computers in people's hands and ensuring they turn on and off.

Let's go back to 1998.

> The Internet has just found its legs. As nonprofit marketers, we are acutely aware that we must have a website that rocks. "Do the web or die." But, to our senior leadership team, it's an expense that seems like much ado about nothing. "We have a website," they said. (Yes, at that time, the measly amount of energy IT was allowed to throw at the concept was technically called a website. But a single page that scrolls and scrolls and scrolls forever didn't cut it then—and doesn't now.)

> My then boss, Dan, shed blood for five years fighting for the funds to build one of America's largest nonprofits a sophisticated website.

Senior management didn't believe the web was here to stay, and they certainly weren't ready to invest in the inevitable future of online donations and event registration, e-learning and electronic communications.

They—along with many other nonprofits—were in denial and slow to fathom the forthcoming shift from print to digital, from the postal service to wireless, and from standing in line to make a purchase to checking out from an electronic shopping cart.

So Dan, being the creative guy he is, came up with a stroke of genius to visually communicate the absurdity of our members' online experience. Using perforated printer paper (the continuous ream of paper with the perforated holes along each side that fed automatically through a dot-matrix printer), we printed out the organization's single, continuous "website" (a.k.a. one long page) and draped it through the ceiling tiles across the building's entire twelfth floor. The paper-streaming river flowed a ridiculously long way. It was dramatic and compelling. Dan's brilliant stunt got us permission to build a real website.

Is your nonprofit keeping up with and staying ahead of the curve of where technology is headed?

Millennials, born during this technology revolution, currently consume the majority of entry- and mid-level jobs in the nonprofit workforce. They have little to no patience for devices that are slow or inefficient, and rely on wireless connectivity to access data and files anywhere, anytime. Give this generation the right tools, and they can work miracles.

No more one size fits all.

Additionally, people's patience with mass communications is ending. The rising expectation is that you get to know people as individuals, and communicate efficiently and effectively *with* them rather than *at* them. No longer can you simply build a one-size-fits-all communication system or flood constituents with one-sided banter. **To know me is to love me.**

Consumer-driven content and niche marketing demand that newsletters, magazines, thank yous, emails, letters, solicitations, and all other interactive communication show that you *know and care* about the likes, dislikes, passions, hot buttons, giving and membership history, data, et cetera, of the individual you're reaching. If I love horses, don't send me stories about dogs. If I've sponsored ten kids for ten years, don't send me a form letter that thanks me for supporting only [fill in the field Johnny]. For that matter, don't send me ten individual thank yous for each kid I sponsor, either! If I am single and gay, don't send me newsletters filled solely with photos of heterosexual moms and dads and youth programs.

People want to see themselves as valued and cherished partners to your nonprofit. If I want to ensure clean water on Earth, don't pitch me a bunch of stuff about saving the rainforest. If I'm 34, married with children and donate money because I really care about protecting freshwater for future generations, don't dump my name into a communication stream that talks at me about hummingbirds and spotted owls. And nothing will bug me more than repeatedly sending me an appeal for money when I just gave you money, asking me to rejoin when you never asked me why I quit, or inviting me to be a member when I already am one.

Disconnects do more harm than good.

Technology is further changing how nonprofits advertise. Most nonprofits, and even blue-chip charities, have never had advertising budgets and have relied for decades predominately on public service announcements (PSAs). But as people shift their TV habits to viewing recorded shows that omit ads or ad-free shows viewed on a mobile device, the traditional nonprofit TV-PSA will become obsolete. In the near future, PSAs will be too expensive to produce and distribute for the few remaining TV watchers. Instead, such video productions will move to a digital release. As fewer and fewer people read, newspapers go by the wayside and information is distributed digitally, in tight, concise bites. Video will grow as the most prominent form of communication, promotion and advertising for nonprofits. Digital production crews will replace press release writers and magazine editors.

On-air advertising, however, will not cease. Nonprofits will aggressively get into the game of product placement— the skill of embedding your brand, logo or message within the script or storyline of major motion pictures or television programming. For example, the television show *Brothers & Sisters* airs a scene in which characters Kitty and Justin discuss having her kid write a letter to Santa as part of Macy's *Believe* campaign (for every letter dropped off, Macy's will donate $1 to the Make-A-Wish Foundation).[12] The Macy's shopping bag subtly adorns the kitchen counter as Kitty shows her brother the full-page promotional ad during the characters' casual conversation. The pitch verbiage was perfectly and naturally embedded.

No one stopped, looked at the camera and said, "Hey folks, this is a PSA!"—but to a trained eye, it was a brilliant product placement effort by Macy's to benefit both itself and the Make-A-Wish Foundation of America.

Meanwhile, technology's influence on how money moves is impacting the financial transaction involving membership, donations and program fees. Money is now mobile and global. In the past, I couldn't deposit a check into a bank branch of the same institution across state lines. If I wanted cash in Europe, I had to find the sole American Express office to physically convert U.S. dollars from my credit card account into foreign currency. Today, ATMs are the cheapest and easiest way to get foreign currency throughout the world, and can move money internationally via computer and phone. Face it, if I can now pay a taxicab or street vendor using a device plugged into a smartphone or make a purchase through a kid sporting an iPad, then I'm sure as heck not going to wait in a registration line to sign my kid up for youth sports, find an envelope and stamp so I can snail-mail a year-end donation, or call to request my tax-deductible receipt.

Emotion provokes donations.

The race now is to capture funding instantaneously using mobile money. Recently, while in San Francisco, I was approached by a young man decked out in UNICEF garb (a.k.a. canvassing). He was thrilled I'd heard of the charity. He shared photos on his tablet of efforts to end the preventable deaths of children, and proudly showed me his smartphone, explaining he could process my contribution right then and there. "You'll have your receipt in an instant; it's a speedy process," he beamed. Capturing people's commitments at the peak of their emotional connection works. And technology now enables us the ability to ask and act—in the moment. Mobile money is changing the course of fundraising significantly.

No longer can we afford to invest in messages that reach our target audiences, ignite emotion, compel action but drop off in a call-to-action that waits for them to get home, reconnect with the feeling, and (if we're lucky) act. The expectation that money can be moved instantaneously is the new norm.

I don't need to tell most people about where technology is going or its dire relevance. It's obvious if you open your eyes. But I can confidently tell you this: the gap is widening between the nonprofit haves and have-nots. Those nonprofits—big or small, rich or modest—that invest in technology will surpass all others. I predict this will be the single most important determinant as to a nonprofit's strength or weakness. Those organizations with the best infrastructure to capture and earnestly engage supporters by tapping into their hearts, minds and souls will ultimately win.

IT "HELP" DESK

16

THE JEKYLL AND HYDE BOSS

*"I must admit that I personally measure success in terms of the contributions
an individual makes to her or his fellow human beings."*

Margaret Mead

I've worked for some really fantastic bosses in my career, great coaches, super managers, and ultimately, lifelong mentors. Like most people, I've also worked for some real doozies.

One boss was a Dr. Jekyll & Mr. Hyde. Dr. Jekyll could charm the heck out of board members and major donors. In fact, a primary reason I took the job was because he came across so charismatic during my interview. After my hiring, however, I met Mr. Hyde—his dark side and alter ego.

In the safe confines of the office, Mr. Hyde would regularly appear, screaming and cursing at the staff ruthlessly. You could see it coming. His face would turn bright red and his otherwise soft eyes would grow huge and buggy.

Then he'd blow.

Anna has been the executive assistant for fifteen years. She's seen more than four CEOs come and go. She's a classy, sophisticated, hard-working woman in her late forties who has her job down pat. As I walk to the copy machine, I notice Anna on the phone—eyes wide open, filled with panic and fear. Our eyes meet and immediately I read her beckoning for help. I approach her desk, and she puts her hand over the phone receiver. She whispers, "He's in his car, lost on the west side. He's going ballistic!" She returns to listening, and tries to offer assistance.

As she's cut off, she pulls her ear back from the phone, and I can hear the shouting voice from my position.

Anna's eyes well up as her posture deflates. She holds the phone an inch from her ear, just listening and shaking her head slowly back and forth. He won't stop yelling. He won't listen.

I extend my hand, offering to take the call. Anna's eyes are grateful as she hands me the phone.

"This is Jennifer. Give me your cross streets!"

He curses some more about how stupid his assistant is for giving him the incorrect directions. I repeat my question. Eventually, I am able to give him enough information that he locates his destination, and slams the phone down.

At this point, I'm shaken, but pleased it's over. I know he'll return to the office later acting like nothing ever happened. It's his modus operandi.

Mr. Hyde turned out to be one of the most challenging figures in my career.

I've prepared the final membership campaign artwork and scheduled an appointment to ensure he's comfortable with the messaging before it goes to print. I enter his office, and find him light-hearted and jovial. He inquires about my weekend and shares a bit about his. We review the creative. The copy looks good to him. I breathe, relieved we will make the press deadline. Yippee. I thank him for his time and prepare to leave when he adds, "…However, I don't like the colors. You need to change them."

I'm taken aback. I wasn't expecting him to assume the role of creative director. He's never cared about that before.

I explain, "We're using the same color palette the team chose for this campaign six months ago, in order to keep consistent…" The veins on his neck begin turning as purple as his shirt. His nostrils flare. I notice and quickly backpedal, knowing that, in situations like this, anything but complete compliance is futile.

"I told you to change it, now change it, dammit!" he barks while slamming his fist on the desk.

That night we're at the board meeting. I observe as he works the room, shaking hands, flashing his big smile, bellowing his big, gregarious laugh. He had the volunteers eating out the palm of his hand.

"What a chameleon!" I think to myself, "If they only knew."

Each staff member endured his wrath, although the timing and target was unpredictable. We had all become accustomed to the drill: exit his office with your tail between your legs, absorb the wave of pity coming from your colleagues, slither away to the confines of your office, and lick your wounds in private. Come back tomorrow for another day.

He managed to run every good staff person out of the place. Within a year, 85 percent of the senior staff had quit, transferred or gotten the hell out of Dodge. So much talent literally blown right out the door. Unfortunately, the only way a CEO can be fired is for the board to take action. But the board of directors is comprised of community volunteers who, frankly, have their own jobs, lives, families and issues to contend with. The last thing they need is a volunteer headache. They love helping with a positive lift, but dread getting their hands dirty in either a mud pit or a blood bath, if they can avoid it. Hence, many bad CEOs stay too long.

My philosophy is that you never leave a place until you're sure you've learned all that you can. So, I spent a lot of time practicing how to maintain perspective and keep my emotions in balance. It was easy to allow this one person to make my life miserable. Mr. Hyde could show up for only ten minutes, yet I'd spend the entire evening griping about this guy to my family. One day, my life coach gave me a brilliant exercise. She said, "draw a grid box with four quadrants (+) on a piece of paper. In the upper left quadrant, shade in how much negative energy you get from your job." I used my pencil furiously to scratch in the entire quad. Next she said, "think of the positive energy you get from your job and fill in the lower right quadrant." I shut my eyes and thought of all the amazing children we serve, my wonderful colleagues whom I respect and love so much. I thought of their camaraderie, their shared suffering, their dedication to the mission… I colored in the entire quadrant, once again. The next question stopped me cold in my tracks. "In the lower left box, write down how many people are contributing to the negative energy of the upper left quad."

"Whoa," I thought. "Really only one. Just one bad guy giving me all that negativity."

I correctly anticipated the next question, "and in the upper right box, write down the number of people you receive the positive energy from."

I guesstimated roughly 25…maybe 30…"Well, if I include some of the members…and volunteers…oh, and the corporate sponsors I work with, and the staff at the mayor's office…" The number kept growing. At that point, I understood clearly the point of the exercise. The good overwhelmingly outweighed the bad.

But I was giving the bad all the credence. I used the image of this exercise to balance myself whenever he began commanding too much of my energy. I pushed the negativity down, reminded myself the perpetrator was one person, and refocused instead on the abundance.

This tactic helped me survive for a year and a half. I was blessed with the opportunity to practice my craft of nonprofit marketing and corporate sponsorships for this particular organization, and I learned a great deal, including how NOT to manage.

Once I felt like I had learned all there was to learn from this venue, I tendered my resignation. You can't change another person and if the board won't act, the CEO isn't going anywhere.

So you have to move on.

Eventually, the consequences of the 85 percent staff turnover started reflecting in the financials. Membership had grown flat and fundraising revenue was down. It was years before he left, but the damage had been done. Lots of lost talent, significant recruiting and retraining costs, and tremendous disruption of productivity. It took years for the new CEO to rebuild the momentum and recreate a team.

I have three takeaways from this experience:

1. **Keep things in perspective.** Dead, negative weight is heavy while positive energy and love is light and airy. Don't let the negative weight pull you under. Stay focused and enveloped in the light-heartedness of the positive.

2. **If the board of directors won't act, you will probably need to move on** when you're ready. Bitching, complaining or being miserable only hurts you, your family and your friendships.

3. **Don't leave a situation until you've learned everything you can from it.**

Finally, an important note to those who serve on a board of directors: When you have ridiculously high staff turnover, look closely at the big guy! Ensure that the organization has an exit interview policy. The public reason people typically give for leaving isn't the truth. It's only meant to maintain class and not burn bridges. Someone who has the trust of staff needs to be empowered to ask, point-blank, the true reason behind each departure, to connect dots, look for trends, and prepare quarterly summaries (with anonymous measurements) for the board.

When it becomes evident that rampant turnover is the result of a CEO, the board must act.

It's no fun to be a volunteer board member and have to get involved in the underbelly of nonprofit staffing—but ensuring the vitality and health of the organization, and that the right captain is at its helm is perhaps your most important responsibility. People's lives can't afford for you to look the other way.

NOTE TO SELF: If there's high staff turnover, examine the big guy!

JEKYLL & HYDE

17

WHEN MARKETING WAS A FOUR LETTER WORD

In the 1980s, I was continually corrected when my mouth uttered any word deemed "too commercial" for nonprofit use. One such taboo word was "marketing."

"Nonprofits don't market," I was told. "We *communicate*." Hence my title, director of communications (a.k.a. marketing).

I was hired to get the word out, to distribute press releases, engage with media, place PSAs, manage special events, and create brochures and marketing materials. Then, like any good nonprofit, the bosses realized I could do more than just that. Pretty soon I was running membership campaigns, designing direct mail, creating advertorials and launching a corporate sponsorship initiative. I missed a meeting once and found myself in charge of the switchboard.

"After all," my boss quipped, "aren't telephones a form of communication?"

While management wanted me to communicate brilliantly so that membership, program enrollment and donations would rise, there was also a distinct fear that the materials shouldn't look too slick or professional.

"No one will donate to us if they think we have too much money," was the typical explanation for why the flier or newsletter should look crappy. Hence, we got florescent green fliers copied on the mimeograph machine, brochures photocopied onto pink paper with the image slightly crooked then trifolded by hand, posters with the date and time handwritten in chunky black marker.

Here's the trouble with that kind of thinking: people—who might give you money—want to support an organization that has its act together, knows how to raise funds, and delivers quality results. Image and reputation are often all your donors will ever know about your organization.

"Let me ask you this," I once said to a group of nonprofit program directors. "In terms of your own children, the most precious people in your life, do you want to leave them in the care of an organization that looks like this (I held up a crappy flier) or this (I showed them a beautiful four-color brochure graciously underwritten by XYZ corporation)?" I turned to the philanthropy directors and asked, "If you work your whole life and want to leave your estate to charity, do you leave it to one that seems to have never seen a dime (crappy flier) or one that has enjoyed support from others (beautiful brochure)?"

Hands down winner: folks want the shiny penny. It's like picking a stock broker: you want him to be successful enough to look like he knows what he's doing, but not so well-off that he appears to be part of a Ponzi scheme. Yet the reverse is also true—if you come across a financial planner wearing Dockers and Keds, driving a Subaru, you run for the woods. Packaging is important. Marketing matters.

Similarly, fear that the charity may be unable to meet the increased need, phone calls, inquiries, volunteers and requests for services often leads to an internal desire to diminish promotional efforts. (Albeit the fundraising goals are set higher than previous years.)

"If we are too successful in marketing, then we might get more work than we can handle."

"Too many people will find out about us, and we don't have a budget to ramp up our services."

While there may be some truth in these statements, they are not rationales for why you should not do marketing. Fear shouldn't shut down your marketing; it should inform it. Marketing done well is concentrated around specific objectives, target audiences and outcomes. It has a specific call-to-action and is designed to strategically impact a defined goal. A well-built plan is not created in isolation, but considers all ramifications and possibilities. You plan for success.

Healthy nonprofits are those with which people are excited and engaged. Enthusiasm brings fundraising, membership and volunteer support, a.k.a. engagement. Engagement brings the resources needed to fuel the mission work. It builds upon itself.

Design your strategy to drive awareness, coupled with an increased "ask" in fundraising, a robust infrastructure ready to accept new supporters, and pre-determined strategies for growth when met with evidence of increased demand. Prepare for success, and you will prosper.

This leads me to the most important marketing principle of all time: the best way to kill a bad product is to advertise it.

Think ahead! Is there anything awkward, embarrassing or inappropriate looming inside your organization? Consider the obvious landmines: executive compensation, incident reports regarding safety, program vs. fundraising ratios, revenue and expenses vs. measurable impact, 990 filings, et cetera. Also consider the internal health of your organization. If staff is miserable, leadership corrupt, operations dysfunctional, programs lack quality, or financials are in disarray, then think twice about launching a major national media or marketing campaign.

Media, cynics and regulators love to look under the hood. Get your house in order before you shine a spotlight on it.

While no charity is perfect, we must be competent and confident. Thoroughly assess your potential skeletons, fix or diminish them, and always arm yourself with a proactive crisis communication strategy. Anticipate any tough questions the media might ask. Pre-determine and vet your responses. Be prepared to explain why any challenge may exist, the organization's position, what is/isn't being done about it, and provide some key facts and sound bites. Don't be a deer caught in headlights, and know that "no comment" is not an acceptable response. Better to be prepared under the gun than to run defensively.

Finally, examine the underbelly of any marketing messaging you're going to pump before release. You can try to drive program registration by touting that you have the very best swimming program, but if you've had two drownings in the past five years or only 11 percent of participants signed up for a second class, you're putting a bullseye on your chest.

When you say you are the best, people are more apt to want to find your flaws. Kathy Lee Gifford was known to boast repeatedly on her talk show about her perfect children, perfect marriage and devoted husband, Frank Gifford—until someone found thrill in proving that untrue by tempting Frank with a knockout flirt. Similarly, former New York State Attorney General and Governor, Eliot Spitzer, earned a reputation as one of the toughest, strictest AGs in the country until 2008 when *The New York Times* reported that Spitzer had patronized a high-priced prostitution service, leading to his resignation.[13]

When you place yourself on a pedestal, people enjoy knocking you off.

A local nonprofit teams up with one of the hottest ad agencies in town to create a series of print PSA ads for its annual support campaign. Instead of simply doing the work and releasing the ads, the agency puts out a press release and thumps its chest about how revolutionary the creative work is. They don't put the spotlight on the charity, the mission or the fundraising call-to-action. Instead, they focus on their own creative brilliance. With these remarks, the agency stuck its head out in a way that teases media and watchdogs to turn over the rock.

A reporter at a metropolitan newspaper takes a peek when he receives a call from a man who is upset with the agency positioning of these "faces of poverty and need."

"She's not a bum," the caller exclaims. "She's my mother. She got paid to do that ad!"

Under the rock, the reporter discovers that the people in the print campaign—positioned to reflect the faces of need in the community—are all actors. The story breaks that the charity has misrepresented its ads and claims.

Lots of charities use actors and models in their ads. So do businesses. If you think spokespeople really use the products they're hawking, you live in Wonderland. Using actors or models often makes sense. Sometimes, it also makes sense to use real members, donors and recipients. Make the decision on a case-by-case basis, and then **tell the truth.**

One can never be sure why something blows up in the media. I suspect, however, had the agency never beat its chest with press releases about how talented they were, nothing would have come of it. Never let your agency spin a PR campaign for its own benefit, branding and business during the launch. It draws too much attention to the craft of advertising. Let the campaign do its job, and then celebrate success.

NOTE TO SELF: Clean out your closets BEFORE you spotlight your house.

NONPROFIT MARKETING

18

GO WHERE NO MAN HAS GONE BEFORE

Many nonprofits throw staff—with no experience in marketing—into the adventure of growing membership, promoting programs or generating corporate relationships. It's baptism by fire. To make the coals even hotter, rarely are they given a healthy budget to toss at the problem.

Question: *How do you market with no money?* (This really is the million-dollar question; it's also the secret behind a successful nonprofit marketer.)

Answer: *Get very granular and extremely creative.*

Look for the nooks and crannies where the lazy people with deep pockets didn't look. It's relatively easy to open a checkbook and place beaucoup bucks behind a media buy, putting ads in traditional venues with proven track records. Nonprofit marketers don't have big checkbooks. We have to use our imaginations, creativity, negotiation skills and assertiveness.

This is where the term "grassroots marketing" comes from—you run around in the weeds. You don't think TV, radio, print ads, billboards. You think coffeehouse corkboards, grocery store bags and church bulletins.

To get Holly elected, I knew I had to blanket the high school with her name. We could hang posters on bulletin boards or metal posts throughout the school, but no tape could touch the wall. The school administration didn't want paint damaged. Those were the rules. On your mark, get set, go.

Okay, posters and typical signage were a given. Check. No-brainer. I delegated this to the poster committee.

"Push further," I declared. "We need to be smarter." I stood in the hallways of the school, looking for inspiration. How could we blanket the school without touching the walls? Those rows and rows of lockers sure provided a lot of space, I thought. But students have to be able to open them. I kept thinking.

Then lightning struck.

I asked mom to drive me to the store, where I purchased ten rolls of accountant calculator tape. (Note to millennials: calculator tape was the roll of long, thin, continuous paper that an accountant would use in an antique device called an adding machine. The machine would print a strip of numbers out as you added, so you would have a copy of your calculations.) I handed the rolls to the volunteers and told them, "write, 'Vote for Holly...Vote for Holly...Vote for Holly'... until you run out of paper. Use different color markers. Add confetti, stars and other decorations to brighten it up."

We took the rolls to school. Beginning at one end of the lockers, we unrolled and taped it along the metal strip that ran along top of the lockers. The paper ticker tape went on, and on, and on. We covered the three floors of lockers throughout the school. When we were done, there was no doubt in anyone's mind: Holly was running for president.

I took this lesson into my nonprofit marketing career: **go where no man has gone before.** (Well, okay—go where everyone has gone before, because you need to be in the obvious locations, too. Remember, we made posters for Holly, too, but we didn't rely solely upon that typical tactic.) Look for the open space. Find all the nooks and crannies, the unique and overlooked "real estate" through which you can communicate your message. Think of a take-out pizza box as a distribution channel for a flyer; movie previews as a broadcast venue for a PSA or a slideshow; store windows and doors as places to affix a static cling; locally-bottled soda can panels as space to advertise an upcoming event; a vinyl-wrapped taxi or delivery truck as a mobile billboard; a large employer's cafeteria as a place to engage and educate employees; a busy town road and its light poles as a venue for overhead banners, et cetera.

Think physically, digitally, virtually, audibly and visually. Keep pushing further.

NOTE TO SELF: Penetrate the nooks and crannies where your target audience works, lives and plays.

"No resources, mate!"

19

SPRAY AND PRAY MARKETING

Is it a myth or a legend, that if you throw spaghetti against the wall and it sticks, it's done cooking?

I am not much of a chef, so I won't make a decisive ruling on this, but as a long-time marketer, I have seen this theory applied to marketing: throw out a bunch of ideas and see what leaves a lasting impression or stands out on top. Instead of calling it spaghetti marketing, we call it "spray and pray" marketing.

Spray and pray marketing is when you release a whole bunch of PSAs, ads, brochures, fliers, press releases, digital marketing, events and other promotions, out into the enormous marketplace without a target audience, strategy, consistent messaging, success measurements, and plan. You spray and then you pray it works.

Nonprofits notoriously don't have deep marketing budgets. In fact, most have none. So you have to get smart with the few resources you have. **You can only afford one target audience. Choose.**

I was tasked with building enrollment for our nonprofit, after-school child care programs. We had dozens of after-school centers all over the metropolitan area, and we knew our primary audience was parents of kids between six and eleven years of age. Consider this audience: female. Crazed in the morning, getting herself and kids ready and out the door. Drives like a madwoman so that everyone is on time. At work all day, breaking her neck to pick the kids up on time, cursing traffic and evening rush hour the whole way. She gets home and works job number two, preparing dinner, baths and bedtime stories. The next day, the routine starts all over again.

Would newspaper ads reach her best? I envy the mother of small kids that reads any newspaper once a week, let alone daily. Daytime TV? No, she's not home during the day and if she is, she doesn't likely need after-school programs. Direct mail? Maybe, but you'd better have a two second message that will grab her as she sorts the junk mail.

Only a postcard (she'll never open a junk mail envelope) appearing repeatedly (minimum three times, over a short time period of time) in her mailbox might pique interest and facilitate action. But this tactic must be bundled with something else…Radio? Yes, you can definitely peg that she is in the car commuting to/from home, school, office and child care site. A captive audience: the dream of marketers.

When considering this particular demographic, I eliminated the thought of buying the midday or evening radio spots. Her radio is off. Instead, she is most likely commuting weekday morning between 6:00 and 9:30 a.m. and early evenings between 4:30 and 6:00 p.m. I ruled out the morning because I don't have that much money, and she's pressing to get to school, and then to work; she's not thinking about after-school care. So, morning is out; too many distractions. Instead, I focus on the evening commute, 4:30-6:00 p.m., a smaller timeframe. This mom likely starts out in the car alone, leaving work with the pedal to the metal trying to get to the child care site on time. She wants to avoid the dirty "late look", kids on the curb or the nasty $5.00 per minute penalty charge. In this zone, she's captive, thinking about the kids, the child care program, perhaps cursing why the site isn't open later, or milling over the complaint from her kid this morning about how boring it is. Your 60-second ad comes on. Bullseye. You offer an alternative, and she is intrigued by the option. You spent your money wisely. Now, couple the radio buy with the series of direct mail postcards and social media campaign and you have a decent strategy.

Good marketers drill down to find when and where they can capture their target audience, and analyze the most cost-effective way to engage in a conversation with them.

Marketing isn't about how many people see your message. It's about how many of the *right* people see your message consistently. And ultimately, whether you can get them to act or not. Marketing 101 says it takes three times in three different places to make an impression. This means a target consumer needs to see or hear your message once on the radio during her drive to work, once the next day in the grocery store aisle, and once on a postcard seen while flipping through the day's mail. When a person sees a message or brand three times in three different places packed in a tight punch, the belief is that the campaign is *everywhere*. The repetition breaks through and captures attention.

On the other hand, if you think mailing one postcard or letter is going to have an impact, think again. Save your money. People may see it. They may think positive thoughts about your charity for a millisecond. They may even set it aside with good intentions to call or send a check. But it falls by the wayside and is quickly forgotten.

LOGO SOUP

NOTE TO SELF: Only through repetition do you move people into action.

20

CREATIVITY: A BLESSING AND A CURSE

When you are hired to a new job in the for-profit world, you are indoctrinated into the brand identity. Brand guidelines are like religion; you know them and you follow them.

Would a Nike employee dare to change the "swoosh" to a "swirl"? No. He'd be shot.

How about switching Target's red and white bullseye logo to purple and white? No. No one would eat lunch with you for a year.

For-profit businesses invest heavily in their trademarks and maintain tight command and control over how they are used. So why, in the nonprofit world, are these valuable marks constantly tweaked and tampered with?

Nonprofits are notorious for butchering Branding 101 guidelines. The mishmash of brochures, fliers and annual reports—so varied that they couldn't actually be from the same charity—is commonplace. The creative habit of changing logo colors, adding new design elements, and chapters that developed their own slogans and campaigns—so much so that a business person flying from one town to another could see no consistency between the same charity's efforts—is typical.

When I was with YMCA of the USA in the 1990s, we examined the strength of the Y logo. Turns out, the traditional black and red brand mark was one of the most recognized logos in the world, up there with Coca-Cola and Nike. Don't mess with success, right?

Yet, being creative folks, staff at Y's around the country found every opportunity to make it their own. We saw YMCA logos wearing running shoes for fitness classes; logos with apples hung from the Y's "branches" signifying the "deep learning" of Y programs; logos in teal, purple, rainbow colored and neon; and logos with squiggly streamers through the logo, under it, and on top of it.

We counted them up and found we had *164 different versions* of the YMCA logo in circulation. (Don't even get me started on tag lines.)

Have you ever seen running shoes on McDonald's golden arches? Have you ever seen the Coca-Cola logo printed in the color magenta? No, you haven't.*

When it comes to brand identity, **consistency matters**. I often start my workshops by coming on stage dressed in red pants and a yellow shirt. I ask people, "Who do I look like I work for?" Every time, I get precisely the same response: "McDonald's." It's embedded in our brains: red and yellow equals ketchup and mustard. McDonald's. Brilliant. When driving down the highway and I see the golden arches peeking up yonder, I know *exactly* what I'm going to get.

Seeing BMW and thinking the single word "performance" or Disney and thinking "magic"—these are brand attributes that didn't happen by accident. They are acts of brilliant marketers at work consistently. So, too, should it be for nonprofits. We simply don't have enough money to rebrand ourselves every two minutes. (I don't care how big your budget is, it ain't big enough.)

Beating a consistent drum drives power. And awareness. And money.

The sister to *consistency* is *continuity*, and that, too, is often a foreign concept when it comes to nonprofits' collateral material. Sadly, it is not unusual to audit a charity's brochures, postcards, direct mail pieces, annual reports, and newsletters *only to find not one looks like the other.*

Try this test: lay your collateral materials out on a table, step back and ask yourself, "Is this the same organization?" More than likely, you'll find each piece has its own set of colors, as well as its own fonts, layout and tone. The only consistent element is the charity's name, address or logo plopped somewhere on the piece.

This kind of disassociation does serious harm to nonprofits. You are literally spending time and money disconnecting from the community's image of you.

---

* *Some people like to point to Google's ever-changing Google Doodles as a counter argument; but the truth is that Google – and only Google – has established that creativity, and more importantly, the habit of regularly changing its homepage logo. The intent was to have fun, and they succeeded in making that part of their identity. But make no mistake; Google's corporate logo is always the consistent primary-mix-of-colored letters.*

You're all over the board, which conveys unprofessionalism and disarray. As a donor, I don't want to give my time, money or support to something so frazzled.

Get your act together.

Select a color palette that you will use for *all* of your materials. Develop a layout theme that runs consistently through all the pieces. This doesn't mean they all need to look exactly the same. In some pieces, you can pop one color more dominantly; in others, draw from another hue in your official palette. (Imagine walking into a friend's home and noticing that some walls are painted in soft pastels, while others—in the same room—are brilliant primary colors. It might work for her, but guests would probably think of her as a quirky homeowner. "Quirky" in marketing does not bring comfort to potential donors.)

Please don't misunderstand my point about consistent brand identity with not refreshing your creative. No one wants to look at the same brochure year after year after year. And sending out the same looking postcard or direct mail piece to your supporters eventually becomes like bad wallpaper in your house: you don't even notice it any more. Every so often, you must visually refresh, renew and redesign your brochures, website, et cetera. Just remember that while every hotel needs a facelift and every fast food joint needs a fresh coat of paint, make no mistake, the golden arches will always remain golden.

Clarity is another powerful engine of nonprofit marketing. One great example comes from my days with YMCA, and the name(s) we gave to child care. At one point, we counted more than 111 different names for our child care programs: Tiny Tots, KidzCare and 109 other creative twists, all brainstormed by local staff. The creativity was to be admired, but the effort was ineffective.

In 1997, YMCA of the USA began its preliminary work on a national positioning campaign. We did our research, and the results were compelling: parents confirmed that they preferred the straight-shooting, professional nature of the name, YMCA Child Care, feeling it conveyed simplicity, strength and reputation.

Our brains give only a few milliseconds of attention to incoming marketing messages, and in that millisecond, parents could not connect "Tiny Tots" with child care.

Thus began a nationwide struggle to change to a single sub-brand. The fight was internal, not external. Some jumped on board right away, others dragged or dug their heels in deep, not wanting to say goodbye to their clever creations.

It was a tough time but an important lesson: don't expect people to stop and interpret your message. They don't have the time. Say what you mean, and mean what you say: YMCA Child Care.

How do you know when you get it right? Use the person-on-the-street approach—let them be your own, personal focus group. *Before* 2008, if you stopped random folks on the street and asked what service does America's Second Harvest provide, most would answer, "No clue." *After* 2008, when the charity's name was changed to Feeding America, it's a safe bet that most everyone would answer, "Hunger relief." Smart move.

The moral of the story is to say what you mean, and mean what you say: Make-A-Wish. Feed the Children. World Wildlife Fund. Save the Music. Boys & Girls Clubs. Phoenix Children's Hospital.

Be clear. Be consistent. Be persistent. And don't make me guess.

 NOTE TO SELF: Say what you mean, and mean what you say.

CREATIVE BARNSTORMING

21

BRAND PROTECTION IN A WIRED WORLD

A lot of nonprofit organization dialogue these days is around *protecting the brand*. "All we have is our good name, our reputation," is the common rally. True, in many ways. But it's like raising teenagers—if you think you can protect them by locking them in their rooms, you're wrong.

I've been party to many conversations on websites and in online communities that go something like this:

"We should put a poll on our website that asks our supporters what they think of our new PSA campaign."

"What if they hate it? That would be really embarrassing after all that money spent producing it."

"True. Well, what are we going to do about all the complaints we're getting about the event last weekend? People are really upset that the celebrity didn't show up at the event."

"Maybe we should post the letter of apology received from the celebrity stating what happened and pledging half a million to make up for it."

"But if we do that, more people will learn about the situation than just those who attended. What will they think—that we can't guarantee a celebrity's attendance when we sell tickets and tables? That could seriously damage future sales and events. Let's just keep it in the family—we can email the letter to anyone who calls and refund them their money if they ask for that."

The Internet is helping folks voice their opinions, which are based upon one's individual experience and perception. What one guy likes, another gal hates. We've been around long enough to know this, and it's time to acknowledge that consumers are actually smart enough to think for themselves.

You have to be willing to let people speak their truth. If someone has had a bad experience, they may complain.

Another may counter the claim. In the end, the banter works itself out if your organization really is doing the right stuff. You can't please all of the people all of the time. Folks get that and can read between the lines.

Let your supporters support you. Be open, real, earnest and authentic. Let *them* tell your story, spread the word, and pass it on. Let them fight your battles, whenever possible.

The idea that you can control the banter by publishing a few raving testimonials and static data about your organization, and think you're going to mobilize, engage or invigorate your supporters at a moment's notice is foolish. Consumers now control brands, not brand managers. Gone are the days when one could simply create a headline, tag line or PSA that positions your brand the way you want it. Here and now are the days of social media, viral videos and opinionated bloggers. We live in a world now where consumers have the last word.

Instead of being afraid of public opinion, think of it as a gift. You've been given the gift of a spotlight on the problem. Engage the community in a problem solving exercise. Ask them for solutions. Use *them* to fix it. Show them you're listening, that it is a village—and their criticism is valued.

People will ignore frivolously tossed stones. Consumers are actually quite smart and savvy when you give them the chance. Be open and willing to admit your mistakes, receptive to constructive feedback and use it to make continuous improvement, and be willing to let your champions and supporters carry the torch on your behalf. After all, its much more believable when someone *else* says you're great!

 NOTE TO SELF: You can't control your brand, you can only manage it.

NONPROFIT IT

TIPS FOR NONPROFIT MARKETERS

Here are a few nuggets I always share with new marketers:

1. You can't afford mass marketing.

2. Even if you could, it's dead, so forget it.

3. You have to pick one audience, choose your most important target audience and talk *with* them. Only them. No one else. If you find yourself saying, "but everyone is a potential customer or supporter," then slap yourself and go get some training.

4. Wear out your message. Don't waste money on producing new creative (ads, photography, logos, brochures, websites) just because you want something new. Yes, big marketers constantly rollout fresh ads… But you're not them. Stop wasting time creating, and get the good stuff you have out there…repeatedly.

5. Beat the same drum over and over again. Just about the time you're sick of saying it, the public is just starting to hear it.

6. One-way communication is passé. It used to be that a car company put an ad on TV and led everyone to believe they had the safest car on the road. Now, customers post opinions, vote with stars, give out accolades and gripes, blog about their experience, embed links to research or reports that substantiate their claims, release a friend-to-friend viral boycott, protest or letter writing campaign…You can say whatever you want about your brand, but consumers today will set the record straight.

7. You can no longer control your brand. Instead of being afraid, embrace it. Get heavily into social and interactive media because most traditional forms of marketing and communications, except word-of-mouth, will be dead within ten years.

22

REINVENTING THE WHEEL

I love that the local chapter of a nonprofit has the autonomy to manage its own destiny, select programming, initiatives and priorities based on the needs of local constituents, hire staff, adjust finances and customize marketing to reflect the demo- and psycho- graphics of the local community.

Likewise, I love a national office that engages the chapters in defining a collective vision—one that consolidates, builds and delivers the infrastructure, processes, tools and templates for chapters to customize and easily put into practice.

We often analogize large, federated nonprofit structures to that of a franchise system in business. Each franchise is a sole and separate, autonomous unit but operating under one umbrella brand, system and process managed by a franchisor. The role of the franchisor is to protect the trademarks, roll out the know-how, and control the business concept. The franchisee is responsible for carrying out the services for which the trademark is known. If the franchisee goes rogue, the franchisor may revoke the license, yank use of the trademark and withdraw its assets and support. If the franchisor doesn't deliver its commitments under the franchise agreement, the franchisee can sue for breach of contract.

The franchisee knows he/she is a small business owner, an entrepreneur, and the one ultimately responsible for implementing the franchisor's resources and making it work. No franchisee pays all that money to purchase a franchise with the intent or desire to throw out the tools and systems and waste time, energy and money creating each element over again by themselves. So why do many nonprofit chapters, councils, branches and affiliates work to reinvent the wheel?

It's commonplace for local chapters to ignore the national photo archives, instead hiring a local photographer to take pictures of smiling kids and families because *"we want photos of our own, local kids, not generic national kids."*

Really? When the public glances at a magazine ad, do they really care (or notice) whether the subjects are wearing T-shirts with the town name on the pocket instead of the charity's generic, recognizable logo?

Local customization is important, but reinventing the wheel just to say it's a local wheel is a waste of valuable resources. The same conversation applies to the development of PSAs, collateral materials, database architecture, and purchasing.

In addition to our redundancy, we have a bad habit of thinking we're more important to the other side than we actually are.

> I love taking new national staff to tour local chapters. We always get the red carpet treatment because that's just how nonprofit staff rock—classy, respectful and honoring to the national staff (at least face-to-face). During each visit to a local office, I ask one key question of the local representative (Note: not to a senior manager, because they, of course, would toe the party line and answer much differently.) "How many times a day do you think about the national office?" Without fail, I get a perplexed look, like I'd just asked them how many times a day they think about Neptune. I fill the dead silence by asking a follow up question. "Okay, how many times a *month* would you say you think about the national office?"
>
> Still looking bewildered, trying to concoct an answer that is both respectful and honest (remember: these are some of the most honest, good natured people you'll ever meet), they humbly reply, in a soft spoken, apologetic voice, "Maybe once or twice."
>
> The jaws of the national newbies drop.
>
> "Yep," I say to them. "So when you're sitting in your ivory tower at national, cranking out all those newsletters, communiqués, instructions, campaigns, directives, best practices, et cetera, just remember: these folks are trying to fight their own daily fires—and while they want to digest everything you're spewing out, they just can't. They've got a full plate dealing with the local stuff. In their minds, you're a million miles away."

This is the reality. While the national office is drafting global strategic plans, signature marketing campaigns and best practices, advocating issues on Capitol Hill, preparing talking points for the CEO's appearance on the *TODAY Show*, and trying to keep the collective financial ship afloat, the local chapters are trying to figure out how to raise enough money to keep the doors open, how to appease a hot-headed board member, how to get the programs and services to the most needy people, and determine which kid pooped in the pool.

It's Mars and Venus for sure. Both different. Both important. What becomes maddening, however, is when energy and resources are spent fighting each other, reinventing the wheel, jockeying for control and arguing over pride of ownership. Because nonprofits are comprised of human beings, ego will always get in the way. Instead of maintaining focus and grounded intention on servant leadership—that soul-centered belief that we are on Earth literally to serve each other—and giving each other the benefit of doubt, we shift our effort to making our own way, own mark, furthering our own career and satisfying our own ego. When this occurs, we scatter our energy. Our focus is no longer on advancing the mission of the charity, but on ego.

NOTE TO SELF: Fragmentation breaks momentum and derails us from achieving our goals.

"Yes, that's exactly the tire I need.
Now, can you just find me one made locally?"

23

WHAT PROMOTION?

I t's classic. An organization puts tons of effort into launching a membership campaign, driving program enrollment, organizing an event, recruiting for staff or volunteers, et cetera. The promotional materials are distributed, press releases written, entertainment hired, the volunteer committee organized—everything is a go—except for the communications with the frontline staff.

"Thank you for calling the Nada Foundation. How may I help you today?" answers the cheerful switchboard operator.

"Yes, I received a letter in the mail asking me to support your Kids Campaign. It says my donation will be matched by a corporate sponsor if pledged before July 31st. Who is the corporate sponsor and since tomorrow is the 31st, can I send in a check or will it arrive too late for the match offer?"

"Ummmm, I'm not familiar with that campaign, sir. Ummmm, let me put you in the voice mailbox of our fundraising director. She's gone for the day, but I assume she'll know more about it," the operator responds.

"But if she's gone, then it will be too late for me to mail the check..." replies the potential donor.

"Well, I'm afraid I don't know anything about that campaign or the letter you received. Let me put you on hold, sir, and see if I can find out the answers to your questions. Hold, please!"

The operator pushes the hold button and begins her quest for answers. She becomes frustrated knowing that, once again, they launched a promotion with the switchboard phone number in case of questions, but she has nothing on it.

She's armed with no information and looks like an idiot. She hates looking like an idiot.

Turns out, there is no one in right now who knows the answer, so rather than telling the caller what he doesn't want to hear, she opts for the easy escape route: voice mail.

Meanwhile, the potential donor is on hold, listening to the looped voice recording telling him how great this organization is. He rolls his eyes, thinking if the promotion was so great, the charity would have its operator up to speed.

He glances at his watch. Two minutes. "Come on...seriously?" Suddenly, a voice comes on the line: "Hi, you've reached the voice mailbox of Mary Martin, director of fundraising for the Nada Foundation. I can't take your call right now..." Irritated, he hangs up.

Remember that the folks who answer your phones, work your reception desk or manage your switchboard are continuously drilled by questions from callers who expect them to have a clue about stuff being promoted and advertised in the public arena. Arm them with knowledge. Get them the info!

Think about how many times promotions don't look like they were effective. I've heard folks blame poor choice of zip codes, ineffective call-to-action, pricing issues, and the economy. Of course, any one of these things could be a culprit. Too often, talented marketing staff do everything right, but the organization comes up short. Great marketing plans are executed. The creative is dynamite. The budget is generous and well placed in the media. The campaign drives the intended target and interest right to the front door or front lines (via phone or website) of the organization—but from that point on, you witness a massive drop off. Why?

If the guard at the gate doesn't know you are coming, he simply won't let you in.

When you're knee-deep in planning a campaign, an event or fundraiser, you often assume everyone in the organization is tuned into such a vital component of the organization's budget and goals. They are not. Folks are busy doing their jobs, and as part of yours, you need to ensure communication regarding the project you're managing. The adage "the devil's in the details" is true. You've got the obvious stuff covered; it's the not-so-obvious that will bite you in the butt.

 NOTE TO SELF: Arm the front lines with information.

"Our current promotion? Uh-uh...let's see...
Let me just make a quick phone call..."

24

START WITH THE MAN IN THE MIRROR

I begin my training session asking, *"Who is in marketing?"*

A few hands go up.

"Who here is in fundraising?"

Far fewer arms extend.

I offer that by the end of class, when I ask those same two questions again, I expect each and every person's hand to rise.

If you work for a nonprofit, you certainly have an area of expertise: human resources specialist, accounting clerk, lawyer, IT guru, CEO, grant writer, volunteer coordinator, youth counselor, executive assistant, data processor, program coordinator, social worker…whatever. But no matter what your job title says, **you are also in marketing and fundraising**. Why? Because you can promise to do the most incredible mission work in the world, but without money and resources, your charity is washed up and you can stay home in bed.

People get really nervous when I suggest they be marketers and fundraisers. Lots of people don't have a creative bone in their body and just as many equate asking for money on par with root canals.

But the simple truth is that we are all marketers, and we do it every day.

Marketing is simply the art of connecting people. In this case, it's about connecting your organization (comprised of people with a passion) to donors, members, volunteers, sponsors, media, and the public-at-large (a lot of people with similar passions).

In our personal lives, we send marketing messages every time we put a note in a child's lunchbox or send a birthday card to a spouse. When you wave to strangers as they drive, you're sending a message. The color of your house's front door sends yet another message.

At work in a nonprofit setting, it's delivering first impressions by answering the phone positively and professionally, sorting out a customer's dilemma without getting defensive, or showing up on time to a Rotary Club meeting, that *matters*. It's the style and condition of your shoes, your timeliness, grammar and punctuation in your proposals, handwritten thank you notes to people who have helped you, your smiles, pleases and thank yous. It is how you talk about your charity on airplanes, among friends, and at your kids' school.

Marketing is how we package ourselves as representatives of the charity and convey our genuine desire to people in the outside world that they matter and that we earnestly care about having a relationship with them.

We're all marketers.

Similarly, **we're all in fundraising**. I always tell my kids: it's easy to want money. It takes hard work to earn it. Folks love to place all the responsibility for generating revenue on the fundraising staff. "That's their job, not mine." Well, if you want a paycheck, or want the doors of your charity to stay open, then you'd better change your mindset. It's everyone's job—from staff to board members—to bring home the bacon.

If you're the CEO, you are the chief fundraiser for the organization! Let me say that again. If you are the CEO, you are the *chief fundraiser* for the organization. Get out of your office and go raise money. If you're uncomfortable raising money, you're in the wrong industry.

If you're a board member, your two key responsibilities are to (1) help raise and open doors to money, and (2) to uphold your fiduciary responsibility of ensuring a well-run organization.

Most nonprofits can only afford to pay one person to wear the marketing title. Similarly most fundraising departments consist of one or two people. It's not uncommon for the same person to wear both hats. Yet the expectations of generating tens of thousands of dollars and millions of impressions while cultivating hundreds of trusted relationship cannot be placed solely on the shoulders of a few people.

- If you're working an event and hear a supporter griping about something the charity's done, tell someone! Give the organization the chance to right the wrong before it looses a valuable supporter;

- If you hear someone mention they're trying to decide which charity to name in their will, politely figure out who the person is and give the development staff the lead;

- When working the front desk and a member is angry, it's your job to find a solution;

- If you notice the telephone recording has outdated information, it is your job to notify the person in charge of it and encourage an update;

- If you see promotional materials for a program that has passed, remove them. Nothing shows staff apathy more than a bulletin board or kiosk filled with outdated information.

When everyone contributes to putting the organization's best foot forward, and remain alert to opportunities where people are interested in deepening their involvement, then all boats rise.

❈

Caution:

Most people are terrified of asking for money and don't want any association with the responsibility. So telling people they are fundraisers might not get the results you want. Instead, explain that they are all "fundraising connectors", and that you need them to be the organization's eyes and ears—listening for, seeing, and stewarding opportunities to strengthen relationships.

NOTE TO SELF: No matter what your job description is, if you work in a nonprofit, you are part of the marketing <u>and</u> fundraising team.

SINGING THE SAME TUNE

25

DON'T REFUTE THE PIE

I have a T-shirt in my closet that I take out periodically for amusement. A chapter executive made it for me to drive home the jab we'd had going between us for months. The front of the shirt read *"Don't Refute the Pie."*

The back was adorned with a pie chart that showed total philanthropic giving annually in the United States. The largest slice of revenue, is the $217.79 billion that comes from individual donors. His point: that my work in corporate giving, cause marketing and sponsorships was the measly, minuscule slice of the pie, only $14.55 billion.[14]

Send link to Legacy Music Fdn

"Point noted," I would quip. "It's a small slice of the whole, but a rapidly growing slice. Besides, I still think we should take our fair share of that $14.55 billion."

"Nope," he would bellow, *"You can't refute the pie!"*

I'm a lover, not a fighter, so I allowed the banter to continue throughout my tenure with the organization. Frankly, it didn't matter much whether he liked corporate relations or not. He happily cashed the check for several million dollars that came from the national office each year, and did a good job of stewardship. So, I just returned the pokes. (Once, I sent a Marie Callender's Boston Crème pie to his hotel room during a conference. The note read, "Welcome to Phoenix. Enjoy the pie.")

We were friendly about it, but two things really did irk me about this nonsensical joke he'd invented for our relationship. First was the minor but obvious point, that he was insulting me by insinuating my work was worthless. More annoying, however, was that he didn't understand the evolution of corporate relations, strategic philanthropy and corporate social responsibility.

He couldn't see the future.

No matter how I tried to explain, it didn't matter. To him, it was and always would be a sliver. Yet that "sliver" brought in tens of millions of dollars annually to the organization. It was—and is—one of the fastest growing pieces of the pie. More importantly, this "slice of the pie" is not measured accurately. When done well, corporate relationships between nonprofits and for-profit involve not only cash contributions, sponsorship fees, foundation grants and in-kind donations, but also advertising, PR and media muscle, visibility, retail shelf space, impressions, volunteers and committee members, employee giving, customer education and engagement, experiential marketing and pro bono product placement opportunities, significant purchasing discounts, knowledge sharing, loaned professional services, introductions to vendors, merchants, business partners, agencies and other potential partners, royalty income, and so on. Only cash and in-kind commitments are considered in the official pie, but all the other benefits are there, and the value is real. It is support that plays a critical role in igniting the brand's visibility, power and value.

In this world we live in, nonprofit brands must remain top of mind to be viable. You need the marketing muscle of corporate America and small businesses to stay relevant. And frankly, it's better to tap the generosity and willingness of business in co-ventures than it is to spend hard-earned donor dollars trying to market yourself.

Oh, and one more thing: the "Don't Refute The Pie" argument failed to recognize that the work in corporate relations and the marketing power it brings to an organization only makes it easier *to raise money from individuals.*

When writing your will, you aren't likely to leave the money to an organization you've never heard of. When thinking you'd like to volunteer somewhere, you start calling the charities that come immediately to mind. When you see a disaster on TV and you want to help, you're going to reach out to those you respect and believe will do good work with your money.

I don't refute the pie. But like every good stockbroker will preach: diversify your portfolio. Build a variety of revenue streams and don't put all your eggs in one basket. So as long as children and crayons can "Create-A-Pepper" at Chili's restaurant in just four short weeks and raise $8.2 million for St. Jude Children's Research Hospital, I will continue to enjoy my slice of heaven. [15]

26

CORPORATE RELATIONS AND MARKETING GO HAND-IN-HAND

My favorite college professor, Wolfgang Deckers, is a bright-eyed, brilliant German who taught me International Political Economy at London School of Economics. His style was much like Robin Williams' character in the movie, *Dead Poet's Society*. He would enthusiastically beat his desk, infusing our brains with the truth that politics and economics can never be separated.

"Whatever the economic situation, there's a political consequence. Whatever the political decision, there's an economic impact. They're always connected, always intertwined. You can't have one without the other," he said.

In nonprofits, the same applies to corporate relations and marketing. Corporate relations, sponsorship, cause marketing, strategic alliances—whatever you call it—is based in marketing principles. It's not philanthropy. The company isn't involved solely to be holy. Expectations exceed a thank you note and charitable tax deduction. Corporate relations are contractual commitments between the two parties, with each legally pledging its assets, resources and efforts to achieve specific goals. They are win/win, mutually beneficial alliances. The best ones are built around shared value.

It takes the whole village to deliver against these contractual obligations. It takes buy-in, commitment and effort from a cross-section of departments, including legal, program, accounting, events, IT, research, and marketing.

And the greatest of these is marketing.

Frankly, you can stumble through the implementation with every department except marketing. Marketing is the heartbeat of corporate relations.

Without the deep-seated buy-in and delivery from the marketing and communications staff, corporate relations is dead.

I'd just crafted a strategic alliance with one of the nation's largest magazines and contractually secured over $4 million worth of ad space in the magazine. **Guaranteed.** Not PSAs, remnant space that only runs if and when they had a blank page that hadn't sold. This was a donation of *guaranteed ad space*. We just had to provide the full-page, camera-ready artwork.

During the four-month negotiation to secure the deal, our vice president of marketing (the department in which corporate relations resided) left the organization. Our beloved, enlightened and smart leader who respected the marriage between corporate relations and marketing was gone. Our new vice president was imported from the for-profit consumer products world. She was a skilled brand manager used to working on the task at hand with plentiful budgets. She did not yet appreciate the scrappier mentality required of nonprofits.

She'd been on the job three months when we inked the deal. She was "rethinking" the brand and working with an agency to develop new creative. I welcomed her desire to put her own thumbprint on the brand, and appreciated her desire to get it right, so I asked the magazine to be patient. Give us some time to submit the ad we wanted to use. I stalled.

And stalled.

And stalled.

After six months, it became uncomfortable.

After nine months, highly embarrassing.

After eleven months, a joke.

The magazine signed a one year contract, and kept reminding us, "use it or lose it." We were pissing away an amazing opportunity, and they couldn't understand why. Neither could I.

I pleaded, and begged. I suggested we use an existing ad—one that had worked fine over the past 100+ years of our existence. I got a firm no. The CEO, to whom she reported, chose not to do anything about it either. His bad. My hands were frustratingly tied.

The president of the magazine visited the charity's headquarters. He was standing in the hall when the vice president of marketing walked by. They exchanged hellos, then jokingly but serious, he wrapped his hands around her neck in the choking position, gently shaking her, saying firmly, **"Get me an ad!"** She giggled and responded, "The creative process can't be rushed."

To this day, I replay that response in my head and continue to be flabbergasted by it. The president of a Fortune 500 corporation has his hands around your throat saying he's been waiting eleven months for an ad, and your response is, "the creative process can't be rushed?!"

Yes, it can.

No ad ever ran.

This type of internal mayhem is rampant among nonprofits. It doesn't matter if you're a big charity or a small one. Your ability to deliver against contractual agreements is a by-product of the internal culture, directly related to the commitment and actions of the senior leadership team. Every department must honor its role in the delivery process, and most critical, the CEO and senior leadership must act when systems or people fail to deliver. In this sense it's simple: when you willingly accept millions of dollars from a corporate supporter, deliver what you promise. No excuses.

If you're going to be all hat and no cattle, then get out of the corporate relations game. Save your brand and reputation.

27

THE PINKIFICATION OF AMERICA

I n college, my roommate was obsessed with the color pink. She just loved the color; it fit her personality. Everything she owned was pink. Every T-shirt, towel, washcloth, her hair blower, toothbrush, bra and underwear, her umbrella, raincoat, convertible Bug, her couch, bedroom wall and sheets…even the one she draped as an overhead bed canopy. I was living inside a bottle of Pepto-Bismol.

I have flashbacks every October.

The pinkification of America has hit an all-time high. Everyone from runners and football players to just about every product under the sun, including yogurt, kitchen appliances, running shoes and cans of soup is decked out in pink. When cause marketing exploded in the 90s, consumers hadn't seen it much, and we took it at face value. If the sale of a product triggered a donation for charity, and considered price and quality equal, we thought, "how lovely" and probably chose that product for our purchase. Pretty soon, we had Lids for Kids, Box Tops for Education, Aisles for Smiles and Shop for a Cause. Every charity hastily tried to get in on the act of proceeds to benefit, slapping logos on every product imaginable, owning their own color, and hitting customers up at every cash register. Hungry for its portion of the cause marketing revenue pie, nonprofits leveraged every marketing gimmick possible from yellow wristbands to red dresses and round up campaigns. It worked marvelously when these ideas were fresh, new and exciting.

Nearly thirty years after its inception, this trend of generating money off the backs of the consumers will continue, but consumer fatigue is weighing in. Shoppers are getting tired of being hit-up to add a buck to every purchase or seeing a logo slapped everywhere saying "buy this product and proceeds will benefit." The marketplace has become saturated. The pendulum is swinging.

Consumers are much more accustomed to cause marketing today than thirty years ago, and they are starting to put their glasses on to read the fine print of the disclosure language. Similarly, the states' attorneys general

THE PINKIFICATION OF AMERICA **135**

have also awakened and are putting much more pressure for these deals to comply with consumer protection laws. Hence, the best of the best nonprofits and corporations are complying with the Better Business Bureau's Wise Giving Standards which dictate the precise language that should be used with these promotions to ensure transparency, so that consumers can assess what specific amount of money is actually going to the charity, during what time period, any minimums and maximums, and how one can contact the charity for further information. Those that comply are clearly proud of the relationship and feel good about the fine print. Those that don't, may have something to hide.

NOTE TO SELF: Transparency and authenticity are the cornerstone of a meaningful corporate/cause alliance.

"This just in: The world over seems to have been
dipped in Pepto-Bismol."

28

KNOW WHEN TO WALK AWAY, KNOW WHEN TO RUN

Nonprofits are notorious for having the gracious, "thank you for helping us" mentality. After all, it's a must with volunteers and supporters—a culture of gratitude is essential. But when a corporate donor tries to take you at your lowest price, undervalues your worth, or takes advantage of your weaknesses, that should be a "no-go."

A major international corporation invites me to its world headquarters to negotiate a strategic alliance. The company is a quick-serve restaurant. Employee and customer surveys reveal that affordable child care is the number one issue/concern for its employees and customers. (Not surprising because this restaurant's clientele is predominately working mothers from lower- to middle-income families who cannot afford the booming costs of quality child care in America.) The company pledges to raise approximately $5 million per year. We are thrilled imagining the support.

I always refer to the negotiation stage as "peeling back the layers of the onion" because you have to find out what's at the core of the company's interest. When corporate America talks to nonprofits, they think we want only to hear how much they love our mission and appreciate us. While the sweet talk is fun to listen to, what we really need to know is, "What do you really want from us?" and "How will you measure success when the honeymoon is over?" These essential pieces of information help you determine (1) if you really want your charity to "get in bed" with this particular company, and (2) whether you can meet your new partner's real expectations.

After about two hours of negotiations that day, I finally uncover the crux of their interests: our child care centers need to be referenced as "XYZ Child Care" in all our marketing and communications material. Bottom line, they want us to rebrand our largest program with their company's name.

The corporate senior executive stands up forcefully over my chair and attempts to exert his dominance over me, the little nonprofit gal.

"You will take the deal, if you want our support," he says.

I take a deep breath and rise from the low couch upon which I have been sitting and meet nose to nose with the big bully. "We cannot and will not rename thousands of brick and mortar facilities, give up our own brand identity—one of the most recognized in America—and disregard our donors who committed to those capital campaigns," is my retort.

Never before had I left a negotiation and headed straight for the bar, but I did that day. A scotch on the rocks, as a matter of fact.

Back at the office, I tell my boss what happened, and to expect that we might lose the deal.

There are two reasons I didn't cave: (1) it was wrong—wrong for them to ask, wrong to treat us that way, and the wrong strategy for the betterment of child care in America, and (2) I knew my boss and senior leadership team had my back. I wasn't going to get fired, even though I'd spent months negotiating this multi-million-dollar deal and some pompous jerk derailed the whole effort. I was empowered to say no, and not fear ramifications of not getting the money.

I was fortunate to work for an organization that understood this basic truth: sponsorship sales and revenue goals are lovely benchmarks and certainly give staff parameters to go for, but, what you never want, is to have your people negotiate poorly just to save their own hide.

Two days later, the company's "other guy" called to tell me we were good to go. I asked about the title sponsorship requirement, and he replied that it was off the table. They'd be fine with presenting status.

"Whew!" I thought to myself. "Still have the sponsor, still have my job, and still have a spine. All in all, a good day!"

NOTE TO SELF: Never love a deal so much, that you are not willing to walk away.

29

YOU AGAIN?

How many times can you realistically go back to the same donor well? Apparently, some staff believes the answer is: repeatedly. After all, it's a bottomless money pit.

My phone rings, and I answer. On the line is a colleague, sharing with me the latest and greatest program they've developed. Coincidentally, we announced last week a major sponsorship with a global telecommunications company that took eleven months to negotiate.

"Do ya think the company would be interested in sponsoring this new program?"

"Sure," I think to myself, "let me call them and see if they'll simply add another zero to that contribution they're making. Shouldn't be a problem."

I start my deep breathing exercises because I know I'll get ten more calls just like it.

I get why they're asking. Money seems to be flowing, and they want (need) a piece of it. But seriously, do you think it's a sound strategy to hit up a brand new corporate partner one week after we inked our first major deal together? No. It took us eleven months to strategically identify the precise programs, marketing initiatives, and employee engagement activities that *made mutual sense* for the alliance. We need to find a different sponsor for which the new program makes authentic sense.

The reasons phone calls like this push fundraising and corporate sponsorship staff's hot buttons are:

1. A charity can't repeatedly hit up the same donor/sponsor for money or you'll wear out your welcome;

2. You need to diversify your revenue pool so it's clear that many companies and donors are investing in your mission, not just one or two. You don't want all your eggs in a single relationship basket;

3. It feels demeaning, as if our talent consists merely of shaking trees and collecting the falling money;

4. There's *so much more* to the conversation than, "Hey, we've got great food. Wanna fund our restaurant?"

Event sponsorship enjoyed its heyday throughout the 90s and first decade of the millennium. Companies spent millions sponsoring races and runs, sporting events, festivals, art performances, exhibits, golf tournaments and other random events. The prior practice of corporate philanthropy involved cutting a check with nothing in return. Sponsorship became the way of supporting the community while also gaining visibility, consumer and employee engagement and exposure for the brand. Charities got in on the act, selling event sponsorship proposals offering gold, silver and bronze levels. It worked well for that time.

Those days are over because of the reality that it's not a bottomless money pit. Charities started selling their spring golf tournament, returning only two months later to sell the summer bike ride, a month later pitching the fall youth outreach program, and eight weeks later to solicit for their year end sustaining campaign. Nonprofits would repeatedly come a-knocking—wearing out not only the corporate contact, but also the staff. How many times do you want to force a buy-decision, hammer out details, and deal with the lawyers?

The days of selling packaged sponsorships to a single event, program or campaign with hierarchy levels of "gold, silver, bronze" is about over. Isolated opportunities that are here today, gone tomorrow (like a one-day event), that don't connect to other sustainable efforts are seen as undesirable one-offs. They are becoming incredibly hard to sell. And are exhausting!

Instead, the art of bundling is on the rise. A plethora of events, programs, volunteer opportunities, promotions, et cetera that share common themes or programmatic impact are being strategically bundled together in order to provide the nonprofit with a robust arsenal of assets it can offer to its corporate partners. During negotiations, those opportunities that *make sense for the specific alliance* are included.

By bundling what was once a one-off opportunity along with additional, thoughtful activities such as employee engagement, a sharing of internal knowledge and resources, and collaborative marketing, the alliance enjoys ongoing, year-round continuity and momentum that will actually pack a punch and lead to measureable impact.

 NOTE TO SELF: Diversify your revenue portfolio.

"Hey everybody - I think it really is bottomless!"

30

CELEBRITIES AND NONPROFITS

O ne of the most common questions I hear, during the Q&A segment of a training session, is "What is your position on using celebrities?"

My response: "It will make your heart weaker and your patience stronger."

If you've ever sold tickets to a charity event with a celebrity headliner who calls just a few days prior to the event to say he/she can't make it—you know what I mean about the weaker heart. Your heart stops, panic overcomes you, and all you can think is, "*What the hell am I going to do*?"

Maybe they are sick? Maybe something big came up? Maybe they decided to book a haircut instead? You'll never know for sure.

Regardless, nonprofits rarely have a backup plan at their fingertips. Who can blame them? What charity can afford to retain a backup celebrity? You have to take the money from the first failure and turn it into a "Hail Mary" pass. You frantically work the phones, trying to find someone available on short notice. Rarely will it be an A-list celebrity—they don't jump at last minute invitations. Instead, you find yourself eating crow, apologizing to everyone profusely, and praying Plan B won't make the majority of attendees demand their money back. (You will survive because supporters who buy tickets want to see the charity win. But more often than not, your ticket sales fall if you try to pull the celebrity headliner gimmick off again next year.)

I speak from experience.

In my hotel room in New York City, an email from my assistant informed me that our celebrity spokesperson was stuck in Florida due to bad weather, and couldn't get in for the interview tomorrow on *Good Morning America*. Where's my hotline to God? Can't He clear up this storm pronto, for ME? Does someone have a corporate jet? What if she flies out of Miami instead of Tampa? Can she drive all night long or take a train? Oh, right—celebrities don't do that. Shit. What am I going to do? We killed ourselves lining up this interview. Why couldn't she have flown in this morning instead? Oh, right—celebrities don't do that either. Someone get me the aspirin!

We're holding a press conference in New York City with our celebrity diva expected to show up at 10:00 a.m. We've planned a morning media event so that the TV news stations can air it on the noon segments, as well as in the 5 and 6 p.m. news. Cameras are rolling. Everyone from the CEO to the child award recipients has spoken. We're running out of speakers and she still isn't here. My cell phone contact tells me she's still in her limousine—only a few blocks away. How long does it take to go a few blocks in New York City? Apparently 1½ hours. We wait. We punt. We put on every speaker we can think of. The media only really cares about Her. We know it and they know it.

Finally, at 11:30 a.m. she arrives. The media frenzy begins. She struts through the door with sunglasses on, hair teased up and sprayed, lipstick perfect and a skirt that's shorter than short. Cameras flash and reporters leap onto chairs as she makes her way to the stage. She delivers her lines, finished the photo opps, and it's over. At 11:40 a.m. After a whopping ten minutes, it's a wrap. Why do I do this to myself, I wonder? Because that's how you play with the stars.

My nonprofit is filming a new PSA at 10:00 a.m. We are thrilled because we've gotten a hot, A-list celebrity to appear in the TV commercial. The script has been approved. The production crew is on-site. The celebrity shows up at 8:30 a.m. The children will arrive at 9:30 a.m. to be in the background of the shots. All is looking good.

The celebrity sits down in the hair and makeup chair, and her artists go to work. And go to work.

And go to work. And go to work. It's now 2:30 p.m. The children are either asleep on the floor or running around hysterically. Their moms are giving us the evil eye. The camera crew is pissed.

This I know for sure: even after fussing with hair and makeup for two hours, most people still look the same. But you don't say that to your celebrity. For celebrities, you wait (and typically, you wait for hours, not minutes). It's just what you do.

And that's why your patience gets stronger.

There are pros and cons to celebrities. Sometimes it works, sometimes it doesn't. Some celebrities are angels. Others are a nightmare. The bottom line: celebrities are a gamble and you need to know your comfort level with gambling. If you can take the pressure, then roll the dice and be clear about your reasons for enlisting celebrity help.

Research shows us that a celebrity won't necessarily help you raise money, but a celebrity can be an important boost to your brand image. Much like the shampoo in the grocery store, it may not make me buy a bottle right away, but it could cause me to pay more attention to the brand name, particularly if it's a celebrity like. In these United States of Hype and Sound Bites, that can be a very good thing. A celebrity can:

- Lend a degree of credibility (if you're savvy enough to get them, you probably have your act together);

- Help you gain media interest and coverage, especially if you can offer the "money shot" or exclusive access;

- Help get better placement for a public service announcement (PSA);

- Slightly increase donations, because some people will pay more for a wake-up call from a celebrity, a backstage meet and greet, or an autographed event poster.

The next question I get is almost always, "What's your position on paying celebrities?" This question is highly controversial and gets a lot of people's juices flowing. Here's my take (and you may agree or disagree): if your charity is going to have a celebrity serve as your spokesperson, telling people how great you are and how much they believe in you, you should not pay them. Paying a fee makes it seems as though you're buying their endorsement. You're not a shampoo or a beer company, you're a charity and people need to believe you're real and authentic. (And if the public were to find out, they wouldn't forgive either you or the celebrity.)*

There is one exception to the "no paying" rule. If you ask a celebrity to clear her/his schedule to appear at a specific time and place—like a media tour in New York or a press event in Atlanta—you should plan to pay their expenses and make a donation to the celebrity's own charity or foundation in return for the commitment. Often, celebrities will donate this gift back, but it allows them to justify the booking with their publicists, managers, agents and business stakeholders.

I'll go one step further: In addition to donating his/her time to record PSAs, write letters and provide testimonials, a celebrity spokesperson with credibility and integrity **should also make a financial contribution**. I wholeheartedly agree that the donation of time, imagery, testimonials and name is extremely valuable, but if you are the face of the organization who asks other citizens to support the cause, you need to put your money where your mouth is. As with board members, the celebrity needs to have "skin in the game", and open up his or her wallet before asking others to do that same.

Finally, using a celebrity as a booked entertainer is not the same as engaging a spokesperson. If you're hiring a celebrity to guarantee a performance for an event that you will sell tickets to and promote, you need a formal business contract that includes a fee schedule and a cancellation/damages clause. It's a business deal, and you need to guarantee their availability to those who pay to see them, and not rely on generosity. If they want to be generous later, have them donate the fee back to you after they show up.

31

CHOOSING A CELEBRITY

Some nonprofits hang their hat on one spokesperson, like Boys & Girls Clubs of America did in the 1990s with Denzel Washington, or MDA did with Jerry Lewis. Others keep an array of celebrities in the mix to appeal to diverse and multiple target audiences.*

A multi-celeb strategy reduces your risk of:

• A Hertz/OJ Simpson fiasco in which your celebrity destroys his image and dings yours;

• Limiting your appeal to a variety of audiences and demographics;

• A last-minute bailout (The force of many holds them more accountable; you also have built-in backups who can pick up the slack if there is a bailout.)

Clearly not all nonprofits have the ability to attract multiple celebrity supporters. Another route is to find an actor who has the skills, voice and appeal that you're looking for, and hire him to be your forever spokesperson. ChildFund (formerly Christian Children's Fund) has successfully done that with film and stage actor, Alan Sader, who has appeared in numerous television shows and commercials, but is really best known for being the charity's spokesperson. Sader appears in ChildFund's print and direct-response television commercials, shown walking amongst the children living in poverty throughout the world.

Local celebrities can be just as compelling as big name entertainers. Think of your community's popular folks: a newscaster, a radio deejay, an iconic business person, a columnist, a well-known food or arts critic, a local pro, college or even well-known high school athlete, or a local comedian.

---

* St. Jude has done this extremely well by ensuring that neither Danny nor Marlo Thomas were ever the sole face of the brand. Instead, we see everyone from Jennifer Aniston to Antonio Banderas to Robin Williams to George Clooney standing tall for the cause.

Lots of movers and shakers in the community can serve as "celebrities'" for your cause. However, do be leery of politicians. Even if they're popular, politicians can polarize supporters and mark your cause with a political slant. Unless your cause has a clear political advocacy/lobbying agenda, or you can "balance the ticket" (multiple politicians from all parties coming on board), then proceed with great caution.

If you don't have any celebrity supporters or spokespersons, don't fret. Brilliant marketers have shown us the power of making the Average Joe into an iconic spokesperson. Frankly, this can be an extremely powerful marketing tactic for nonprofits.

Unilever's Dove brand broke the mold when it photographed six all-American women wearing nothing but their underwear and love handles in its Dove Campaign for Real Beauty. Progressive Insurance's wide-eyed, spunky brunette, Flo, has been amazingly successful as their go-to gal. (I asked my 11-year-old daughter, "What's that woman's name?" Without hesitation, she answered "Flo." Yikes! Brand marketing at its finest.)

Finally, look for a brand ambassador within your own organization. The Nature Conservancy successfully uses its lead scientist, Sanjayan, as its national spokesperson. He's the Dr. Sanjay Gupta of the environment. Who ever imagined a lead scientist on Letterman? But he's really that good.

Maybe it's a staffer, a volunteer or a member—but look throughout the ranks. You may be surprised to find a spokesperson amongst you. You can create a character(s) that represents your brand, just like the big boys do. If the law of attraction is real, then letting local Jane, Dick and Spot tell your story may just prove to be a smart marketing strategy.

The flip side to this scenario is that the celebrity *does* show up. You sell tons of tickets because everyone wants to see his/her act and the dough rolls in. Victory! Just be sure to have a solid contract in place if money is exchanging hands and you're counting on their appearance to raise money.

If you're faint at heart, go with a really great theme or band instead.

Media still wants the compelling photo shoot or the celebrity interview. Without some hype, your feel good human interest story often falls flat on the editing room floor. For this reason alone, celebrities are often beneficial to nonprofit marketers. But choose wisely. Ask around, and never hire anyone who has a reputation for being difficult or challenging, no matter how big of a star his/she is. Plan for disappointment. Have a backup plan.

NOTE TO SELF: Stay away from the nightmares. They're never worth it.

32

EXAMINE YOUR STYLE IN THE EYES OF OTHERS

If you believe your purpose in life is to learn, grow and evolve your soul—then our jobs give us an amazing opportunity. Being aware not only of another's management styles, but your own, is a key learning.

My boss takes me for a celebratory martini, my "prize" for exceeding my revenue goal by 160 percent. We're sitting at the bar when the conversation flows into his true purpose for bringing me here.

"I'm driving a steamroller, kid. Either you're on the steamroller or you're part of the pavement," he warns. "What's it going to be?"

"Well, I really don't feel like being pavement, sir," I respond, wondering how this man's wife lives with him. "What exactly is it you want me to do?"

He asks that I pledge my loyalty and start feeding him information about what staff is saying about him around the water cooler. He wants to know who is and isn't on "his side."

"I don't want anyone challenging my authority," he informs me.

I'm a 24-year-old kid, not an FBI agent. Asking me to be the locker room narc seems horribly inappropriate. Any ounce of respect I have for the man dissipates.

I understand the concept of being in the right seats on the bus. I've read the book. I get it. I agree that staff needs to be united around the vision, row in the same direction and each have their role. I also support reporting fraud, dishonesty, theft, potential coups, assassinations, and blatant insubordination. But after that, I have always imagined it as a *team* bus, where you can respectfully debate or disagree without getting thrown underneath.

Riders each have their seats of expertise, but should also freely contribute helpful tidbits, such as *"I know a faster, easier route"* or *"Hey, driver, wall straight ahead."* Should a staffer decide not to be on the bus anymore, we would safely pull over, let the person off, thank him for his service, and be on our way. I've never pictured a bus filled with social workers throwing it in reverse, plowing the staffer into the pavement.

> The boss continues to enlighten me about his self-proclaimed management style: "It's like being the owner of racehorses. You find the best racehorse available, run the hell out of 'em, and when they drop, you get another racehorse." I sat in disbelief thinking, "while you might *think* that, why on earth would you *say* that?"

I don't know about you, but I don't find being run into the ground either endearing or inspirational. Neither do most people I know in the nonprofit sector. At heart, we're mostly social workers—born nurturers who have sacrificed much (bonuses, commissions, incentives and stock options) to work for the cause. We don't find crops and whips inspiring. We respond to hope, vision and soul.

But what did I expect? His hero was George S. Patton Jr., the eccentric, controversial and outspoken U.S. Army officer best known for advancing further, capturing more enemy prisoners, and liberating more territory in less time than any other army in military history.

For our staff retreat, he literally came dressed as General Patton for the portion in which he delivered a speech about his goals and vision for the future. It was a sight to behold.

> "I am a soldier, I fight where I am told, and I win where I fight,"he says, quoting General Patton, standing in front of the room in a tan military uniform, an official-looking general's cap, with a raised baton in hand.[16]

> No one says a word. People stare silently, mouths agape. The air fills with deadening weight. "Does he really think this is motivating to nonprofit, social workers?" I wonder. Clearly we were all thinking the same thing: he just doesn't get it.

Just as the steamroller doesn't motivate staff, neither does the spinning top.

I think of myself as an Energizer Bunny. I always have ten irons in the fire. I love pushing my limits, and try to accomplish more in a day than most people do in a week. It's how I'm wired. Rarely, do I meet anyone who can run circles around me. I met my match when the organization hired the new director of corporate relations.

The guy is on steroids. When you leave a meeting with him, you need a three-day nap. You're exhausted from trying to drink out of the fire hose. You reflect on the conversation; you're quite sure you never got a word in edgewise.

Staff tried to work with him, being good sports and even better team players. Each one of us grabbed our baseball mitt, attempting to catch every ball thrown.

"Hey, I just met the CMO of Target. I think there's a deal there. Get on that!"

"I just heard GE is going to open a new plant in Beijing. We should make something happen with that!"

"I'd love to go after a partnership with media companies. Start calling around and see who's interested."

"We have a board member in Kansas who is friends with the wife of the man who is the CIO of Dell. Let's see if we can get some computers!"

"I just met with the president of the United States. He's on board!"

I thrive on creativity, but also on productivity.

He believed his role was that of a chief cheerleader, idea generator and door opener. This might have been great had the staff understood the strategy—a game plan—with defined roles and objectives. Instead, it was a free-for-all power jam with chaos rocking out in every corner.

Staffers are excited to follow the leader, just not off a cliff.

He was a busy bee, generating tons of ideas and swirling the energy. He buzzed around, making noise, but not getting much accomplished. No infrastructure existed to support his wild hair efforts.

This creative, energetic soul thought he was being helpful, but in truth, he was simply ineffective and a drain on the staff's energy. It seemed to the staff that there was no method to the madness, at least none they could understand, articulate or leverage.

The staff worked feverishly, going through the motions, trying to keep up. But in truth, they were paralyzed. Once the director's honeymoon wore off, staff began discounting him. They learned to swallow the fire-hose water or spit it out, focus on what could be accomplished, and ignore much of the ambient fireworks (a.k.a. noise). When a team figures out the leader is firing blanks, brave new leaders rise up. Just like the old adage predicts, in the absence of leadership, leaders are born. They will try to craft a strategy, attempt to bring clarity to the nightmare—while trying to manage and control the superior, keeping damage to a minimum. They pray nightly that he'll move on in a few short years.

In both of these cases, these leaders could have gotten out of their own way, addressed their shortcomings, and evolved their own styles. People want their leaders to be successful and they'll give you the constructive feedback to make improvements, if you're willing to look, listen and learn. But most of us don't really have such guts.

But if you do, the information is there if you're willing to look hard at your audience. Leaders examine the body language and energy in the room when you are speaking. Does staff light up when you walk into the room? Are they genuinely enthusiastic, engaged, sitting up, participating and offering contrary points of view? Or are they tuned out, turned off, slumped down in the chair, doodling, looking deflated or disengaged? Also, look beyond actions for truth. Have people learned it is safest to keep their heads down, wear a mask of compliance, don't rock the boat?

The lesson here is for each of us to remove our self-imposed blinders once in a while, and see what we don't want to see about ourselves. **Take a real, hard look at the audience looking back at you.** It's courageous and valuable to open our eyes and receive the energy—good or bad—and put the information to work, evolving our own selves.

33

TOO MANY PRIORITIES

The word *priority* means "something of the highest importance." Most of the time, only a few things can be the *most* important. Sometimes we even put the word "key" in front of it, to make the point stronger. But what is that magic number? Three? Five? Ten? Fifteen? Where is the tipping point between key priorities and a laundry list?

Personally, I'd say five or less…and certainly no more than six items.

Yet, it is not uncommon for nonprofits to unveil a five-year strategic plan that identifies 15 key priorities, each articulating six lofty, measurable goals, each being obtained by achieving a myriad of subset initiatives. Additionally, each department is asked to identify its B.H.A.G.s (Big Hairy Audacious Goals) for the year. None of the documents are connected in any way.

Board committees and task forces are then almost continuously launched to explore the feasibility of additional efforts. The CEO has the strategic plan; the COO has an annual operating plan; marketing has its communications and PR plan; fundraising has its campaign strategies; IT announces its technology initiative for the digital age; and on it goes. Everyone's saddles are blazing. Things really get crazy when year-end reviews and merit increases are based on separate, unrelated measurements.

Ironically, staff and board meetings typically follow an agenda of reports and updates, rather than a dialogue discussing the successes and obstacles in achieving the "key priorities" in the long forgotten strategic plan. If you ask staff or a volunteer what the organization's key priorities are, they look at you like a deer in headlights.

"Which plan or initiative are you referring to?"

All the shiny lights blind us.

It's a common joke among nonprofit workers that the word "no" isn't in our vocabulary. But it's the one word we long for. Pray to hear. Dream of in our sleep: "NOOOOOOOOOOOO!"

We know we could be more efficient, if only someone would say a loud, "NO!" and implement the KISS principle: "Keep it simple, Stupid." We'd be much more productive, too. But KISS is far easier said than done.

The CEO wants a full-day, all-staff retreat. He instructs his senior team to share each department's top four key priorities for the year, and the entire organization would spend the day figuring out how we might help one another achieve those goals.

To prepare, we each submit our department's top four key priorities and his assistant bundles them together and compiles a list with the header: **28 key priorities**.

At the retreat, each director must get up on stage and explain his or her department's key priorities. In the exercise that follows, we gather in small groups to discuss what each staffer will personally do to help accomplish each "key priority." The entire eight-hour day follows this agenda: "key priority" definition/ explanation followed by creation of a massive To Do List by the various departments.

The HR team escaped the day fairly unscathed, as there weren't too many key priorities that required the HR team to mess with payroll, benefits or the like. But (as so often happens) the marketing/communications team had not only had their team's priorities on their To Do List, but every other department's key priorities somehow involved them—design, layout, PR assistance, research data, messaging, et cetera.

Fundraising was also hit hard. Every priority program required finding the money to fund the dream. Suddenly, the fundraising department had 28 new "priority" packages to sell. The IT group wasn't happy either. Every dream required data capture, an additional web page or micro site, and another database to be built.

By the end of the day, the room was filled with a pack of depressed warriors—all shell-shocked.

"How the hell are we going to do all this?" was the general consensus.

"We're already overwhelmed. Our plates are beyond full!" exclaimed the vocal one.

"They can't be serious!" questioned another.

"I need to find a new job," thought several to themselves.

Here's a fact: an organization *cannot have* 28 key priorities. It means it has *no* priorities. While the exercise had merit in laying all the cards on the table, it should have been done at the senior management level, not the staff level. The staff needs the executive team to establish clear direction and focus. It's senior management's job to identify the initiatives that will most efficiently accomplish the goal. Scattering the workload 28 different directions is simply overwhelming.

We didn't share organizational priorities that day. We shared individual To Do lists. Know the difference.

Note to Self: A list of priorities should be short. Otherwise you've got a laundry list.

34

BEYOND THE CALL OF DUTY

"In all things that you do, consider the end."

Solon

It is five days before my wedding and I've taken a personal day to catch up on some last minute details that have been ignored because I had volunteered the past three weekends to train staff on membership sales techniques.

Upon hearing I'd taken a personal day, the executive director calls my home to remind me there was no such thing as comp time.

"I hear you're out today," he announces in an intimidating tone.

"Yes, I have to get a few things done for my wedding on Saturday (which he is attending). Volunteering to teach those workshops the past three weekends and getting the membership campaign launched has given me no time to tie up loose ends. I need just a few hours to tackle some final wedding details. I'll be in at seven tomorrow morning."

"You understand there's no such thing as comp time, right? You won't be paid for today," he clarified.

"No problem," I replied, now pissed. "Dock me."

I hung up, shaking my head in disgust, promising to never volunteer another weekend again.

When there's no appreciation for going above and beyond the call of duty, you learn to never raise your hand again for anything outside the job description.

His phone call saved $96—a day's wages—and cost the organization a talented staff development trainer who worked for free. Petty.

The world has changed from punching a time clock to an expectation that we're accessible 24/7. Today, it's about getting the job done—whenever, wherever and however. Our mobile devices vibrate at 4:00 a.m., letting us know another thought or task has arrived. We get up at the crack of dawn to take a 5:00 a.m. call with China. We race to the airport at 7:00 p.m. in a last ditch effort to catch FedEx, and are expected to take conference calls from our vacation in Hawaii, and spend countless nights in airports, hotel rooms, and board meetings. It isn't 9 to 5 anymore.

Flexibility around this newfound, 24/7, "always on" world is key. Sometimes, the fact is, life gets in the way of work. Kids get sick. Toothaches flare up. People lose loved ones. Schools have plays during the day. We just need a moment for ourselves.

When work seems to have no problem interfering with life, it really should be reciprocal.

I've known supervisors, like the one above, who write staff up for coming in late after they just worked the weekend; managers who count every sick, personal and vacation day, making sure every hour, half-day and full-day is accounted for when they negate the nights, mornings and weekends spent traveling for business; cultures that make people feel guilty for arriving anytime after 8:00 a.m. or leaving anytime before 6:00 p.m.; and supervisors who frown on anything kid-related during work hours.

What makes nonprofits so attractive to many working parents is just that: flexibility and balance! Smart nonprofits leverage this to attract and retain stellar talent. Those that favor a culture of "butt-in-the-chair" more than "getting the job" done, are typically rigid and stifling. You simply won't get the most out of your team.

Most people who work in nonprofits are deeply passionate and will knock themselves out to do the hard work the world needs. But they must feel and believe their sacrifice is respected and appreciated. Without it, they'll limit their exposure and withdraw inward.

Whenever I see a withdrawn person working for a nonprofit, I look within the leadership for the hammer bearer. If you're the one leading the gauntlet, ask yourself if it's really worth it.

NOTE TO SELF: The work will still be there Monday morning. Enjoy your weekend.

35

INTERNAL CULTURE MATTERS

"We are far more liable to catch the vices than the virtues of our associates."

Denis Diderot

In college, I had two fish, one named Pink and the other Floyd. I loved those fish. I also dug the lyrics they were named for: "Two lost souls, swimming in a fish bowl, year after year…"

I think of those fish each time I see two department heads engaged in a turf war, each jockeying for ownership of a project, a donor, money or control. Each becomes a piranha, protecting his/her "side" of the fishbowl.

"That's our donor. Even though the corporate headquarters is in Manhattan, the CEO lives in New Jersey and he made the decision."

"I am the manager of that relationship. No one calls them without my permission."

"Your branch can't broadcast that radio ad! The airwaves extend into our service area."

"That pledge should get booked in philanthropy, not corporate relations. We've known about that company for years."

"The Internet belongs to the worldwide office. You can't do anything on the web without permission."

I like power and I'm not afraid to say it. Power means you have some control over how your day is going to go. But when leaders in the same nonprofit direct their efforts towards trying to diminish someone else's power, nothing gets done. Or, at least nothing gets done well.

The misperception that internal politics doesn't exist in nonprofits couldn't be further from the truth. In fact, the internal politics can be, perhaps, more intense than in other organizations. I believe that internal politics is a greater drain on staff productivity than lack of money and resources. Even if I'm broke, I can contribute my heart and soul to make the world a better place. If I can't even get out the door because I'm inside fighting dragons, then no positive impact is made. Many nonprofit fundraisers report they spend the majority of their time managing internal politics rather than building and cultivating relationships with their donors. What a sad misdirection of energy.

Many managers subscribe to the philosophy "what gets measured, gets done." True—but be careful where you focus people's energy.

While I agree that clear vision, measurable goals, timelines and defined roles are paramount to great leadership and organizational effectiveness, I hesitate when measurements divide, rather than unite, staff.

Individual goals are great for communicating expectations of each player, but individual goals *in the absence of team goals* force you to work in a silo, compete against your colleagues, C.Y.A. (cover your ass), and protect your territory. When the line of sight is limited only to how you, personally, or your department is performing, it's natural to become hyper-focused to the detriment of the whole.

Nonprofits that have *organizational goals* (in addition to individual expectations) that include *everyone*, the culture tends to be much more collaborative.

Setting the tone that we're all responsible for revenue, not just the fundraisers but folks who open and process the mailed checks, manage the web site's online giving tool, handle the accounting, provide the legal language for the planned gift, keep the technology running—that everyone is working to keep the ship afloat—sends the clear message that we all rise or fall together.

Similarly, collective measurements that pertain to the net profits and ultimate health of the organization being everyone's responsibility are also powerful. Frankly, I love organizations that have a year-end bonus structure for *all* employees based upon the collective financial health of the organization. Even if the payout isn't huge, it sends the clear message that we're all in this together. As an employee, if my annual bonus is based on net profits, I will likely park in the cheap, remote airport parking lot rather than the convenient, expensive garage because it matters to the bottom line.

Culture is the fuel of productivity. A positive internal culture leads to tremendous energy, enthusiasm and productivity. A poisonous internal culture leads to inefficiency, distrust and half-assed efforts.

It is up to leadership to establish the internal culture—and to maintain it.

Too often management turns a blind eye to the infighting. People start making snide remarks, replying with snotty emails, purposefully don't invite someone to a meeting, fill new employees' heads with past baggage and stories about colleagues they've yet to meet (a.k.a. head trash), or participate in sidebar negotiations and passive-aggressive behavior. The sandbox gets ugly and the catfights, deadly.

It is management's responsibility to put an end to it, or better yet, to not even let it start. Create the culture that this behavior won't be tolerated, and back it up with action.

Additionally, management's time gets consumed trying to manage a challenging employee. Valuable time is spent coaching, disciplining, documenting, reframing, and mitigating damage, et cetera. Everyone deserves a chance to turn things around, and managers need to provide redirection…up to a point. When efforts to redirect a toxic employee become all-consuming, it's management's job to pull the trigger. Poison, left to its own devices, will kill the entire joint.

Instead, great leaders establish the boundaries and give people permission to stand up for themselves, to protect the culture, and to shut down the destroyers. It sounds so simple, but the process of creating an internal culture agreement, publishing it, and incorporating it into your hiring, training and management processes has an incredibly positive impact on organizational effectiveness.

You're welcome to borrow a culture covenant that a team I managed once wrote. Everyone contributed to this proclamation, signed it and hung it in their office space. They held me, and each other, responsible for enforcing the "laws." It was as if the weight of the world had been lifted when we were able to identify the nonsense occurring internally. It's a powerful tool—but only if respect, support and, most importantly, enforcement comes from the top.

When leadership backs a culture covenant with action, then it becomes real.

CULTURE COVENANT

With full consideration of my fellow associates, senior leadership, and the chapter network for which we provide our full efforts, I hereby adhere to the following ideals:

1. In executing my daily duties, I will be myself. In doing so, I agree to professionally reveal my unique personality, experience and skills, and will share and appreciate those of my associates.

2. I will proactively explore opportunities to benefit the organization. I have permission to be innovative, and think outside the box of any job description or departmental silo. I am empowered to serve the charity brilliantly.

3. I acknowledge that I will act responsibly and proactively, and make every effort to mitigate reactive behavior. I put to rest past grievances. I forgive and forget.

4. In situations of challenge, I agree to help identify, support, and resolve any issues related to process, ideas, or other needs of my team and of the nonprofit. If I see something is broken or inefficient, I will not assume leadership knows. Instead I will seek to notify, educate and propose solutions.

5. I agree to be receptive to constructive feedback from my associates, and other stakeholders. I will resist in taking things too personally, and remain focused on the business at hand.

6. I seek first to understand, then to be understood. I agree to actively listen and carefully consider the contributions and thoughts of others. Similarly, I will not assume others know my thoughts and intentions, and shall be open to receiving questions of clarification. Likewise, I am free to be inquisitive, and to fact find in order to avoid miscommunication or misunderstanding.

7. I grant to myself and to my associates the right to say "Uncle." This right shall be conferred in situations including, but not limited to, constructive disagreement, consideration of one's workload, and in the sending or receiving of information.

8. I will promptly and effectively recycle all "head trash."

9. I shall refrain from issuing "zingers" and sarcastic remarks that may hurt people's feelings or self-esteem.

10. I will uphold my right, and the rights of my associates, to be spontaneous, have fun with our work, and to *carpe diem*.

Agreed to in whole by (signatures of all team members):

NOTE TO SELF: Leadership's backbone is what defines an organization's internal culture.

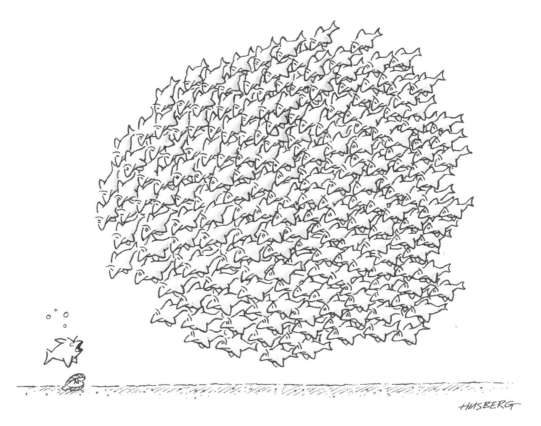

"Look! Louie's got a new, fresh idea. Let's kick his ass!"

36

WHY WE STAY

"'Drinking the Kool-Aid' is a phrase and metaphor, used in the United States and Canada, that means to become a firm believer in something, to accept an argument or philosophy wholeheartedly or blindly without critical examination."

Wikipedia

M ost everyone who has worked any length of time in the nonprofit sector can recite the specific occasion when they "drank the Kool-Aid"—the moment they were hooked and pledged themselves to the cause.

For some, it was when a recipient of services hugged them, tears in their eyes, grateful for the help and support. For others, it happened when an alumnae returned, grown and successful, to tell them they had made the difference; or when they watched a rescued gull, having been cleaned and nurtured, take flight after an oil spill. For others still, it maybe was the poignant dichotomy of seeing a toddler love his newly adopted puppy shortly after walking the long halls of a kill center. It's observing a child draw a picture of his tortured self, a representation of his beaten soul, which commits you for the long haul.

Regardless of where and when it occurs, moments such as these are literally pivotal—they turn you. They turn your gaze, your mind, and your life.

I can personally recall three such pivotal moments. The first was in 1993 when I worked for the Y. I spent a week at a local radio station, recording audio testimonials of our members for a series of radio PSAs. I'd asked the radio station to donate the production studio and crew, and they had agreed. I coordinated with the chapters to gather a handful of members who had amazing stories to tell, and to allow me to interview them. For three days straight, we rolled tape, recording story after story of how people had faced devastating blows in life, and how they believed that the Y made the difference between their success and failure.

Their stories were utterly compelling and powerful. But what moved me most was what the station's listeners couldn't see: the speakers' eyes. Their eyes revealed raw human vulnerability, fragility and strength. As the speakers remembered the pain, their eyes simultaneously teared up and twinkled with gratitude to the Y. This will stick with me forever.

My second pivotal moment was less emotional, but equally affirming. I was walking the back halls of the Coca-Cola Corporation in Atlanta, attempting to negotiate a corporate relationship. While I understand the thrill of the corporate world—generating profits, beating the competition, delivering value for shareholders, dominating the world with your brand—I can't emotionally comprehend why the world really needs an abundance of beverages or, perhaps more accurately, why the world needs me to contribute to that already sustained effort. This revelation became crystal clear to me when I spotted a sign in the back halls of the Atlanta headquarters that apparently was the rallying cry to the employees, coined by the company's late CEO, Roberto C. Goizueta, during his 16-year reign: *"Our goal is to control the majority share of stomach in the world."* [17]

I tried to digest this vision. The ultimate prize: to make the total ounces of liquid an average person consumes in a day as close to 100 percent Coke as possible. That goal wouldn't get me out of bed every day; it doesn't get my passionate juices flowing. Then and there, I recognized the value, for me, of working for a charitable mission.

The third pivotal moment was walking the halls of the oncology unit at Stanford University Medical Center. In room after room sat a small child, head wrapped in bandages with tubes and machines everywhere, and parents sitting bedside. So many children, sick, fighting for their lives. Yet these children are astonishingly brave and wise in a way that haunted me. I felt compelled to deliver the same fight and stamina they did: no whining or complaining. Just get 'er done. Even now, on any day that I find myself crying into my own coffee over the trials and tribulations of my life, I remember these kids. And I suck it up really fast.

These are the three pivotal moments that kept me working in nonprofit.

Twenty years after I began, despite the headaches, the absurdity, hard work, few resources and, at times, diminished perks and compensation, I wake up every day believing someone was truly reaping the benefit of my effort, directly or indirectly—including me. That's why you stay. Once you "drink the Kool-Aid," it's hard to walk away.

"Here's to your first Kool-Aid, Bob. Cheers!"

PARTING THOUGHTS

*"Never doubt that a small group of thoughtful, committed citizens can change the world.
Indeed, it is the only thing that ever has."*

Margaret Mead

I hope you now realize by reading this collection of stories that you're not alone. We've all frequented "dysfunction junction" and are likely to revisit several more times throughout our careers. The key is to keep a sense of humor and passion by staying close to the purposeful-impact you're making. It's what drew you into the business, and what compels you to stay. We are angels on earth, and what we do matters greatly.

The Far Side cartoon, picturing a cow lying on a psychiatrist's couch, hangs in my office to remind me to keep things in perspective. The cow's eyes are swirling as he confesses, "Maybe it's *not* me, y'know…Maybe its the *rest* of the herd that's gone insane." I can relate.

Remember: work hard and laugh often. It's all just Nonprofit Nonsense.

ABOUT THE AUTHOR

Having enjoyed a 20-year career in nonprofit leadership, marketing, corporate sponsorship and strategic alliances, Jennifer founded The Cause Academy in 2008, a marketing agency that provides training, tools and coaching to foster strategic alliances between nonprofits and corporations to advance a common cause that makes a positive impact in the world.

The Cause Academy provides interactive workshops throughout the year; technological tools to help nonprofits work smarter, not harder; staff recruiting services for corporate relations and marketing professionals; and consulting to an array of nonprofit and for-profit clients. Dedicated to making a purposeful-impact in the world through collaboration and synergy, Jennifer serves as the company's lead trainer and Cause Coach®, helping clients develop strategy, campaigns and infrastructure to support their strategic alliance initiatives.

To remain active in the grassroots of the industry, Jennifer also remains a part-time employee with The Nature Conservancy, negotiating its California corporate marketing and media partnerships.

Jennifer is an author, public speaker, trainer, consultant, wife and mother of two. She is a graduate of Arizona State University with a degree in Political Science—Asian Studies and a minor in Mandarin Chinese. She lives with her family in Scottsdale, Arizona.

ABOUT THE ILLUSTRATOR

Rob Husberg is a multi-faceted artist working in several genres, from the silly to the "serious," and everything in between. Visit his extraordinary portfolio of work at www.artofrob.com.

1. Katie L. Roeger, Amy S. Blackwood, and Sarah L. Pettijohn, "The Nonprofit Almanac 2012," *The Urban Institute, National Center for Charitable Statistics,* accessed August 20, 2013, nccs.urban.org.

2. Katie L. Roeger, Amy S. Blackwood, and Sarah L. Pettijohn, "The Nonprofit Sector in Brief: Public Charities, Giving, and Volunteering, 2012," *The Urban Institute,* September 2012, urban.org/UploadedPDF/412674-The-Nonprofit-Sector-in-Brief.pdf.

3. "Quick Facts About Nonprofits," *National Center for Charitable Statistics,* accessed August 20, 2013, nccs.urban.org/statistics/quickfacts.cfm.

4. Katie L. Roeger, Amy S. Blackwood, and Sarah L. Pettijohn, "The Nonprofit Sector in Brief," Table 1, page 2.

5. Carol J. Loomis, "Warren Buffett gives away his fortune," *FORTUNE Magazine,* June 25, 2006, money.cnn.com/2006/06/25/magazines/fortune/charity1.fortune.

6. Jonathan Reid, "Census ranked Arizona, again, near bottom for per-pupil school spending," *Arizona Capitol Times,* June 4, 2013, azcapitoltimes.com/news/2013/06/04/census-ranked-arizona-again-near-bottom-for-per-pupil-school-spending.

7. "25 Lessons from Jack Welsh," *1000 Ventures,* accessed August 20, 2013, 1000ventures.com/business_guide/cs_change-mgmt_ge_work-out.html.

8. "Google ranks number one on list of ideal employers," *New York Post,* March 22, 2011, nypost.com/2011/03/22/google-ranks-number-one-on-list-of-ideal-employers/.

9. "100 Best Companies To Work For," *FORTUNE,* accessed August 20, 2013, money.cnn.com/magazines/fortune/best-companies/2013/snapshots/1.html.

10. Chris Aryes, "Revenge is best served cold – On YouTube," *The Times,* July 22, 2009, thetimes.co.uk/tto/law/columnists/article2051377.ece.

11. Laura Bassett, "Susan G. Komen Loses Support After Planned Parenthood Decision," *The Huffington Post,* last modified February 2, 2012, huffingtonpost.com/2012/02/01/susan-g-komen_n_1247262.html.

12. *Brothers & Sisters* (TV Show), ABC, Season 5, Episode 10, December 12, 2010.

13. Alan Feuer, "Four Charged With Running Online Prostitution Ring," *The New York Times,* March 7, 2008, nytimes.com/2008/03/07/nyregion/07prostitution.html

14. "Giving USA 2012: The Annual Report on Philanthropy for the Year 2011," *The Center on Philanthropy at Indiana University, Giving USA Foundation* (as cited in "The Sector's Economic Impact," Independent Sector, accessed August 20, 2013, independentsector.org/economic_role).

15. "Chili's 2007 Create-A-Pepper campaign breaks record," *St. Jude Children's Research Hospital,* October 2007, stjude.org.

16. "General George S. Patton Quotes," *Military Quotes,* accessed August 20, 2013, military-quotes.com/Patton.htm

17. Betsy Morris, "New rule: Find a niche, create something new," *FORTUNE,* July 11, 2006 money.cnn.com/2006/07/10/magazines/fortune/rule2.fortune.

Made in the USA
Charleston, SC
15 October 2013